FOOD PATH

WE ARE GRATEFUL TO
KHUDA BUX ABRO FOR PROVIDING US
PHOTOGRAPHS FROM PAKISTAN.

FOR MY BELOVED GRANDCHILD, SEHAR, AND HER NAMESAKE,
MY NIECE, ACROSS THE BORDER WITH THE HOPE THAT MAY
THEY BOTH, AND THE COMING GENERATIONS, TRAVEL
UNHINDERED ON THE GRAND TRUNK ROAD TAKING
DELIGHT IN ALL THAT IT OFFERS.

PUSHPESH PANT

WITH

HUMA MOHSIN

FOOD PATH

———

CUISINE ALONG THE
GRAND TRUNK ROAD
FROM KABUL TO KOLKATA

Lustre Press
Roli Books

INTRODUCTION

The Grand Trunk Road or the GT Road as it is popularly known is best visualized as a mighty river meandering its way over a 2,500 km course transporting on its surface millions of passengers and a mind-boggling amount of cargo everyday. The GT Road serves as a life-sustaining link that has acquired over centuries, since it was first built, an iconic status. It has spawned halting stations/resting places that have evolved into towns full of colour and character, each distinct from the other. It is a symbol of the subcontinent's unity in diversity or other way round.

Politics may have partitioned India and Pakistan but the GT Road rolls on across the man-made border majestically. Like any great waterway this road also has many tributaries and distributaries. It would not be an exaggeration to claim that more than half of the subcontinent's population has its life touched by the GT Road one way or the other.

It was the great balladeer of the Raj, Rudyard Kipling, who had first brought alive the romance of this road for the western audience. In his famous novel, *Kim*, he went into raptures describing it,

'And now we come to the big road…the great road which is the backbone of all Hind…all castes and kinds of men move here. Look! Brahmins and *chamaars*, bankers and tinkers, barbers and *banias*, pilgrims and potters—all the world going and coming. It is to me as a river from which I am withdrawn like a log after flood. And truly the Grand Trunk Road is a wonderful spectacle. It runs straight, bearing without crowding

The 'father' of Grand Trunk Road, Sher Shah Suri.

Indian traffic for 1,500 miles such a river of life as no where else exists in the world.'

Ever since, the name has been familiar to all those interested in plain and fantastic tales of Anglo-India. Even before Kipling's introduction the Grand Trunk Road was featured prominently on all the maps of India published in Europe in the seventeenth and the eighteenth century. Anquetil Duperron, a French traveller, who visited India in the eighteenth century and travelled on this road wrote:

'One frequently encounters in India trees in the shade of which travellers pass the time of intense heat. They prepare the provisions they have carried and drink water from the ponds next to which these trees have been planted. There, one sees the small fruit merchants and vendors of parched rice, clusters of people and horses

from all parts. The tree beneath which I halted could cover with its shade more than 600 people.'

Although almost everyone vaguely remembers Sher Shah Suri in the context of the Grand Trunk Road and some even connect Emperor Asoka with the trail, very few recall that it was the Mughal Emperor Jahangir who planted the trees that grace the Grand Trunk Road and were noticed by the early European travellers.

Jahangir has noted in his memoirs:

'according to orders they (the officials) planted trees on both sides (of the road) from Agra as far as the river of Atak (the Indus) and had made an avenue in the same way from Agra to Bengal.'

Thomas Coryote walked his way from Spain to India in 1615 and the journey from Aleppo to Ajmer

took him ten months. The entire expenses were limited to fifteen shillings. He was known to Indians as the English Fakir. From Lahore to Agra he travelled on the GT Road and was deeply impressed by its quality.

When the power of the Mughals diminished and disintegration of the empire set in, in the middle of the eighteenth century, the delta of the rivers Ganga and Yamuna was repeatedly ravaged by warring armies. The tree-lined avenue was denuded of all its glory. The embanked road suffered neglect and became a veritable nightmare during the monsoon. This sad state of affairs had resulted from raging anarchy. Colonel Sleeman, the nemesis of the notoriously blood-thirsty thugs, has remarked in his memoirs, during the mid-nineteenth century:

'In all other areas of India one can at each stage pitch his tent in a grove,

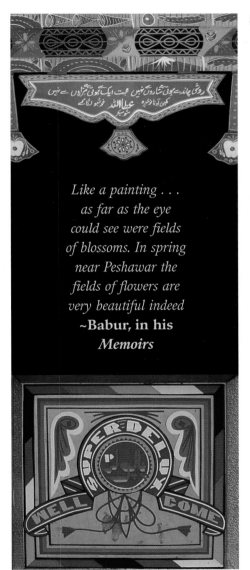

Like a painting . . . as far as the eye could see were fields of blossoms. In spring near Peshawar the fields of flowers are very beautiful indeed
~Babur, in his Memoirs

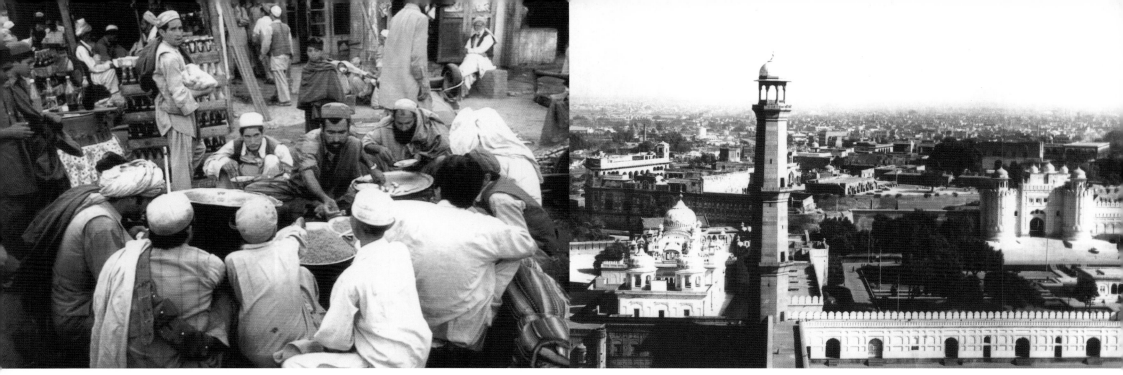

A biryani vendour feeding his loyal patrons in the legendary Qissa Khawani Bazaar in Peshawar.

The cityscape viewed from a minaret of Badshahi Masjid, the largest mosque in Pakistan built in 1674 during the reign of Emperor Aurengzeb.

but in the districts located to the north of Agra, one might make ten marches without ever finding the shelter of a cluster of trees.'

Asoka the Great, we know through his edicts, had ordered that rest houses be built at every eight *kos*. Almost a thousand years after him Harshvardhan of Kanauj had also commissioned the construction of charitable dharamshalas to ensure that the wayfarers never found themselves in dire straits. It was Asoka who according to legend and lore first dreamt of connecting Purushpur (Peshawar) the western-most frontier outpost in his empire with the imperial capital Patliputra by a strategic highway. Asoka, when a young prince, had served along this border and memory was yet green in his mind of the Greek invasion led by Alexander the Great during the reign of his own grandfather Chandragupta Maurya. Interestingly Asoka, though credited with the vision of this pan-Indian highway, may himself have only extended and improved upon a historic route well-trodden before his own birth. In the Hindu epics and *Puranas,* there are references to two major arterial roads— Uttarapath and Dakshinapath. Each road cut a swathe in north and south respectively to facilitate trade and commerce and movement of troops. It is not far-fetched to suggest that the origins of the

Qissa Khawani Bazaar, Peshawar where weary travellers and townsmen were regaled with stories by professional storytellers in the evenings, hence the prefix before the name.

Today the professional storytellers are scarce, their place taken by *chaiwallahs* who are no less loquacious and sell sugary, strong tea by quaint teapots-full.

Grand Trunk Road lie in the intrepid explorations of the Aryans as they spread out west to the east beyond Indus and the land of the five rivers, clearing forests founding agricultural settlements.

GT Road is the backbone that gives physical shape and psychological colour to the racial memories of the majority of the Indian people. On one extremity the GT Road almost touches the sweep of the exotic silk route and on the other it is within striking distance of the ports that open the passage to the aromatic spice route. It is difficult to imagine how many pilgrim circuits have effortlessly been interwoven subconsciously. For majority the father of the GT Road is Sher Shah Suri, the Afghan soldier, who in his meteoric career had ousted Humayun, the son of Babur (founder of the Mughal dynasty 1483-1530), from the throne of Delhi. During his short reign (1540-1555), he initiated wide-ranging administrative reforms, land settlements, and ambitious building projects.

The ground work, it is true, had been undertaken by his Mauryan predecessor in the fourth century BC, but it was Sher Shah who revived and gave a new lease of life to the Grand Trunk Road. Born in Sasaram, Bihar, he too shared Asoka's dream of connecting the seat of his principality with the land of his ancestors. Trees

A lady presiding over the pot at a street-side eatery in Pakistan—a rare sight.

'In every *sarai* he built separate lodgings, both for Hindus and Musulmans and at the gate of every *sarai* he had placed pots full of water, that anyone might drink; and every *sarai* he settled Brahmins for the entertainment of Hindus to provide hot and cold water, and beds and foods, and grain for their horses, and it was a rule in these *sarais*, that whoever entered them received provision suitable to his rank and food and litter for his cattle from the government. Villages were established all round the *sarais*. In the middle of every *sarai* was a well and a masjid of burnt brick; and he placed an Imam and *muazin* in every masjid, together with several watchmen; and all these were maintained from the land near the *sarai*.'

Many of these *sarais* were remarkably beautiful and had a distinct personality of their own.

The Lahore Railway Station, built by the British, with an extensive railway network established in the Indo-Pakistan subcontinent is one of their lasting contributions to the culture of this region.

were planted along the road, caravans and *sarais* constructed and patrolling of the route ordered to stop brigandage.

Sher Shah Suri, according to the chronicler of his reign, Abbas Khan, built 1,700 shelters on the imperial highway.

The *sarai* at the entrance to Agra had vaulted rooms and impressive domes. It could accommodate almost 3,000 guests and provide a stable space for 500 horses. The *sarai* south of Jallandhar, built by Jahangir, was square in shape with each side measuring 165 m, its four corners were decorated with octagonal towers. In 1638, it is recorded, that there were 80 caravan *sarais* for foreign merchants in Agra. The ruins of these *sarais* can be found in Jallandhar, Agra, and Mathura. The stretch of the road between Agra and Lahore was

The Quaid-e-Azam Library in Lahore, a beautiful example of the Raj architecture.

Deep-fried snacks cooked in *kadhai*, a wok-like vessel are popular all over the subcontinent.

quell revolts and rebellions effectively. The road could not be allowed to fall into disrepair. It not only connected the imperial cities—Delhi and Agra—but also linked these with Allahabad and Varanasi—historical pilgrimages for Hindus and fonts of culture.

Things changed when Aurengzeb incarcerated his father Shah Jahan, the builder of Taj Mahal, Jama Masjid and the Red Fort, and imposed an austere code on his courtiers. Much of his time was spent in the Deccan campaigns and the Uttarapath, taken for granted, was neglected. The GT Road suffered and fell into disrepair. The jungle began to encroach on the pathway. By the time Aurengzeb died only the shell remained of the once mighty Mughal empire. Invaders like Nadir Shah sacked Delhi, indulged in carnage and dealt a fatal blow to the Mughal empire. Disintegration followed soon and by the middle of

best maintained and experienced travellers could cover 40 km in a day.

Sher Shah died suddenly in an accident while watching a display of pyro-techniques and this allowed Humayun to make a come back and reclaim his Mughal legacy. As

Humayun's son, Akbar, continued with many of Sher Shah Suri's projects, the Grand Trunk Road grew in significance. Its existence ensured that the emperor could swiftly dispatch punitive expeditions to discipline delinquent and ambitious provincial governors or

the nineteenth century disturbed circumstances made travel along the Grand Trunk Road quite hazardous.

Ghalib, the famous Urdu poet, has chronicled his passage from Delhi to Rampur, providing interesting glimpses of such a journey. One rode on horseback or

was carried more comfortably in a palanquin guarded by a detachment of armed soldiers and had to make arrangements for food and drink along the way. The journey had to be well planned to reach a comfortable camping site before dark. Even beyond Rampur things were not much better. This is where the notorious Pindaris roamed, the ruthless thugs who had been driven away by the legendry Colonel Sleeman from the wild forests of central India. The accounts of Christian missionaries like Bishop Heber and J. Kennedy, protected by colonial troops, reinforce the descriptions of Ghalib.

People understandably preferred to travel along the more secure waterways especially between Allahabad and Varanasi, Varanasi and Patna, and Patna and Calcutta (now Kolkata). Towards the end of the nineteenth century the multi-

A bathing *ghat* on the banks of the sacred Ganga in Varanasi, the religious capital of India.

faceted genius and bon vivant— Bhartendu Harish Chandra and the great Bengali poet Rabindranath Tagore—undertook a number of such river journeys and their travelogues show us how land travel had decayed. The painters of the Raj, the Daniel brothers (William and Thomas) and Edward Lear too have left wonderful sketches, aquatints, and paintings documenting this change.

The fortunes of the Grand Trunk Road changed when the British took control. They wished to eliminate, for strategic reasons, all possible delays that could slow down an army on the march. Their priority was to establish a direct line of communication and transport from Fort William at Calcutta to the farthest frontier outpost. The famous surveys were undertaken with this purpose in mind. Warren Hastings, the first Governor General of India, persuaded his council of building a road from Calcutta to Chunar to be named the

The Lahore Museum, opened in 1894 is the oldest and largest museum in Pakistan.

New Military Road. The idea was abandoned after almost 50 years when work began on an even more direct road through Burdwan. This road was completed in 1838.

There are divergent accounts, travelogues and literary sources that make it difficult for us to plot with any degree of accuracy the course of the Grand Trunk Road in the ancient period. According to the Buddhist texts there was a road, well travelled, that followed the foothills of Punjab and continued towards Mathura along the Yamuna river. When Mohammad Gori invaded India in the eleventh century AD he traversed the course a little further south than the present Grand Trunk Road between Lahore and Panipat. The road shifted again due to imperial decisions in the middle of the sixteenth century. Sher Shah Suri built a fort at Rohtas on the Jhelum and Akbar at Attock on the Indus. Travellers were obliged to cross the river specifically at these points. In this part the road followed the alignment of the present day highway. Originally it seemed that it did not pass through Amritsar.

When the British control was extended to the region of Punjab and Lord Bentinck became the Governor General of India, the

A roadside memorial commemorating the travels along the Grand Trunk Road.

British were quick to recognize the significance of the great road that had fallen into disrepair and disuse. The road was metalled in 1856. Many of the repairs and improvements were under the supervision of James Thomson, the Lieutenant Governor of the north west provinces, who has been described by Phillip Mason as 'the father of public works, in particular the Grand Trunk Road, the Ganges canal and the Engineering Colleges at Roorkie….' Obscure, forgotten settlements in the backwaters in the hinterland—Phagwara, Ludhiana and Jallandhar—were almost overnight turned into pulsating places full of potential and promise. The construction of

Purana Qila, Delhi, in days gone by when the roads were less crowded and the horse-drawn *tonga* did not have much competition.

An aerial view of Connaught Place, Delhi.

a complex network of canals transformed agriculture in the province but it was the road—the one and only GT Road—that made it possible for Punjabis to benefit from this change. What transformed the GT Road was the advent of motorized transport and the decline of inland waterways.

What revived interest in the GT Road was the Mutiny of 1857 and establishment of British empire removing the veil of the Company rule. Strategy and colonial commerce took precedence over all else and overriding priority was accorded to keeping channels of communication and transport open. The Grand Trunk Road was repaired, broadened, and rendered safe for the common traveller. By the time motorized automobile made their appearance the Indian autobahn was ready to receive them.

And it is not only the Punjabis who benefited. The GT Road connected Lahore—the Paris of the Orient—with the rest of the land. In the years before Independence and particularly during the inter war period the GT Road brought Bengalis, Marathis, Gujratis and Madrasis to Lahore and Amritsar and contributed significantly in the evolution of a composite culture.

When the Partition came the Grand Trunk Road bore the painful burden of the traffic of refugees—the helpless victims of unprecedented communal bloodshed, loot, rape and arson. Millions moved in both directions—this perhaps is the saddest chapter in the long history

Qutab Minar (circa thirteenth century) with the Iron Pillar (circa fifth century) in the background standing at the site where the first incarnation of the city in Delhi, Rai Pithora, once flourished.

The rivers served as waterways transporting travellers and goods before motorized vehicles gave the Grand Trunk Road a new lease of life.

of the road. The influx of the homeless—countless separated families had an unexpected outcome. The community kitchen, *sanjah chulha*, centering round the clay oven (*tandoor*) became the essential life-support system of the immigrants. With passage of time the *tandoori* style of cooking would radiate like spokes from a hub and engulf the entire nation in its warm glow. Hole in the wall outlets in earthen huts with thatched roofs began to mushroom along the Grand Trunk Road—the ubiquitous dhabas. It was not long before the dhaba became synonymous with 'great value for money, just like mom's home-cooked, lip smacking, nourishing fare'.

However, one should not be in a haste to conclude that all one can eat along this journey is robust, rustic but tasty Punjabi fare. As a matter of fact, driving along the GT Road one has an unmatched opportunity of discovering the culinary riches of India. With the exception of the coastal and the peninsular one can encounter and savour all the flavours, seductive and addictive ranging from the barbequed temptations of Peshawar and Pindi to piece de resistance of the imperial *dastarkhans* of Delhi and Agra to the delicacies of the Awadh region to subtly sublime vegetarian repast of Varanasi to the tantalizing gastronomic gems of Bengal. The GT Road is the best introduction and irresistible invitation to 'taste India'.

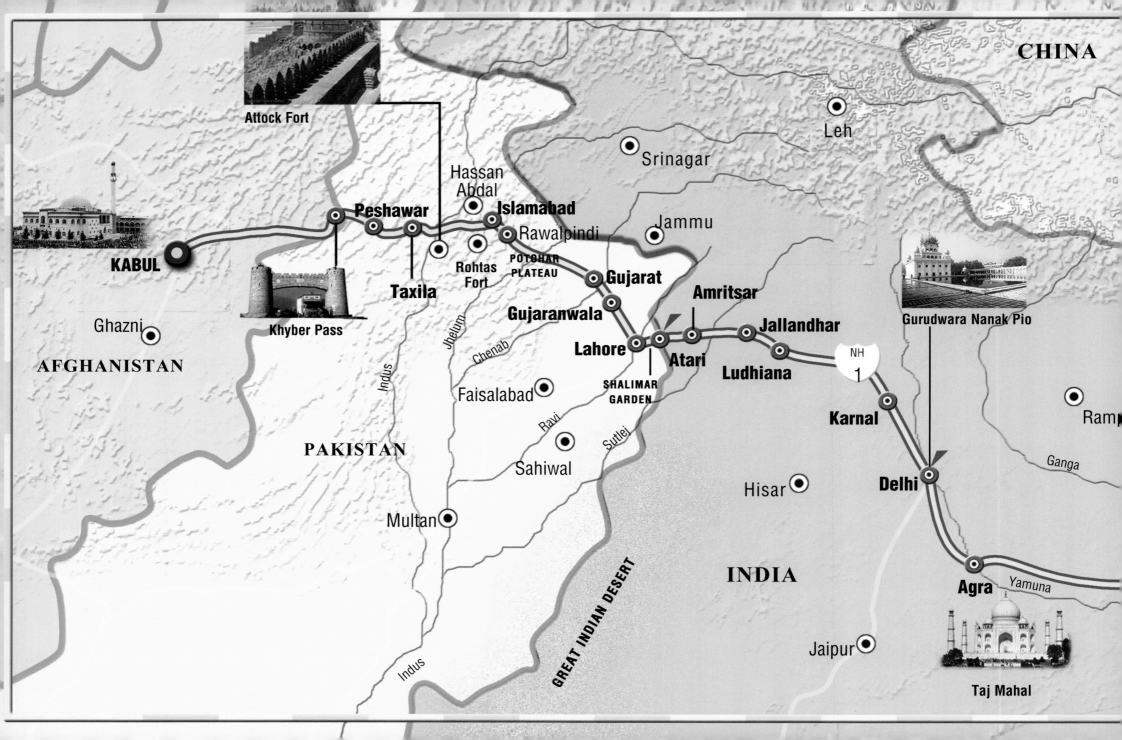

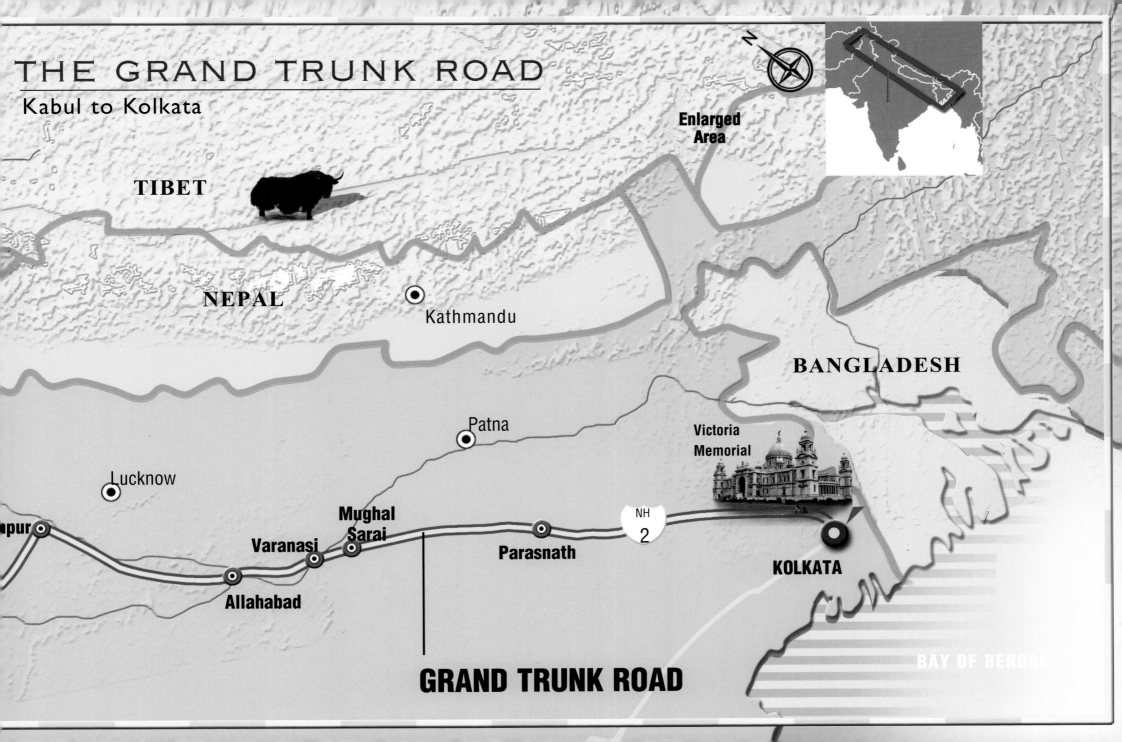

CHAPPALI KEBAB

Food Path: Cuisine along the Grand Trunk Road

DEEP-FRIED MINCED BEEF PATTIES

INGREDIENTS

Beef, minced (*keema*)	I kg / 2.2 lb	Tomatoes	2-3
Eggs	2-3	Green chillies,	
Coriander (*dhaniya*)		finely chopped	2-3
seeds, coarsely ground	3 tsp / 6 gm	Cornflour	2-3 tbsp / 20-30 gm
Pomegranate seeds (*anaar dana*),		Vegetable oil	
coarsely ground	2 tsp / 6 gm	for frying	I cup / 250 ml / 8 fl oz
Dry red chillies (*sookhi lal mirch*),			
coarsely ground	3 tsp / 6 gm		
Salt	I tsp / 3 gm		
Onions,			
finely chopped	2 cups / 250 gm / 9 oz		

METHOD

Make scrambled eggs with 2 eggs and slightly beat the other one. Keep aside.

To make scrambled eggs, heat 1 tsp oil in a pan; add 2 whisked eggs and stir lightly for a minute. Remove and use as required.

Mix all the ingredients together (except oil) including the eggs.

Divide the mixture equally into 10-12 portions and shape them into flat round kebabs.

Heat the oil in large frying pan; fry the kebabs, a few at a time, on medium heat. Cook until both sides are browned. Remove and drain the excess oil on absorbent paper towels. Serve hot with mint chutney.

Kabul is a name that evokes images of rugged wilderness, fierce tribes and, of course, tantalizing glimpses of what lies beyond the fantastic realm of fables and folklore—Persia and Central Asia. This is where many a great journey has begun or ended and this is where one can embark on the legendary Grand Trunk Road. Decades of strife have changed the face of the once quaint city nestling under the shadow of the Hindukush mountains. Today the Kabul river almost mournfully winds its way past buildings, reduced to rubble, and neglected fruit orchards and the stretch up to the international border at Michni Point is strictly for the suicidal traveller.

Kabuliwala

The word *kabuliwala* rekindles memories of the colourful pathan—an itinerant dry fruit trader from Afghanistan—who has been immortalized by the Nobel Laureate Rabindranath Tagore in his famous story by the same name. Like his other compatriots this *kabuliwala* used to visit India every year with sacks full of dried fruits and nuts slung on his shoulders. Some reached as far as East Bengal. The tall fair visitors were synonymous with fierce independence and pride—quick to take offense and not known to forget or forgive a slur.

The North Western Frontier Province (NWFP)—the western extremity where the Grand Trunk Road terminates—merging into an ancient invisible track leading further out into uncharted territory has often been called the 'wild west' of South Asia and it is indeed true that none of the Imperial powers, the British included, ever succeeded in taming the tribals who dwell here. The legendary feuds among warring clans triggered by blood debts accrued over generations have vilified a warm, carefree and very hospitable people. The barbequed fare—the succulent *barra*, *tikka-boti kebab,* and nan are all gifts brought by the anonymous *kabuliwala*. The cuisine of Pothovar—present day Peshawar and Pindi—was enriched by dried fruits like *alubukhara* and *badaam* thanks again to the goodies made available by the guests from Kabul.

GADDA

ROTI SOAKED IN CHICKEN GRAVY

INGREDIENTS

For the gravy:

Chicken, cut into 8 pieces	750 gm
Vegetable oil	1 cup / 250 ml / 8 fl oz
Onions, medium-sized, chopped	3
Garlic (*lasan*) paste	2 tsp / 12 gm
Red chilli powder	1 tsp / 3 gm
Turmeric (*haldi*) powder	1 tsp / 3 gm
Coriander (*dhaniya*) powder	1 tsp / 3 gm
Tomatoes, chopped	250 gm / 9 oz
Salt	1 tsp / 3 gm
Yoghurt (*dahi*)	2 tsp

Garam masala powder	2 tsp / 6 gm
Dry fenugreek leaf (*kasoori methi*)	
powder	1 tsp

For the roti:

Wholewheat flour	
(*atta*)	2 cups / 300 gm / 11 oz
Salt	1 tsp / 3 gm
Butter	1 tbsp / 15 gm
Cooking soda	¾ tsp
Water for kneading	1 cup / 250 ml / 8 fl oz

METHOD

For the gravy:

Heat the oil in a pot (*handi*); add the onions and sauté till slightly soft. Add garlic paste and sauté. Stir in red chilli, turmeric and coriander powders; sauté for a minute.

Add tomatoes and salt; keep stirring. Add chicken and cook on low heat. Increase heat and add yoghurt, garam masala, and dry fenugreek leaf powder. Add 1 cup of water and simmer for a minute. Remove and keep warm.

For the roti:

Mix all the ingredients in a mixing bowl and knead to a smooth dough. Keep the dough covered for 2-3 hours.

Divide the dough into 8 equal portions. Roll each portion into a thin disc.

Khyber Pass has been a mute witness to the vicissitudes of South Asian history. The Aryans are believed to have passed through on their way to the fertile land of the five rivers that was to become their home sometime around 1,500 BC and the Persian forces could annex the adjacent territories to Achaemenian Empire in the sixth century BC only after controlling this pass. The Greeks followed in their wake led by Alexander the Great (326 BC), who dreamt of conquering the world. The narrow and treacherous passage has seen them all—the Scythians and the Parthians, the Mughals and the Afghans—who have been lured by the fabulous wealth of the Indies. Most to plunder and return, some to settle down and leave their indelible imprint on the history of the land.

Heat a griddle (*tawa*) and lay a disc flat over it. Cook one side till lightly brown. Turn the other side and cook again till lightly brown. Remove and repeat till all the rotis are made. Shred them into small pieces.

Mix the shredded rotis with the chicken gravy. Serve hot with lemon wedges and garnished with green coriander and garam masala.

RED CHILLI CHICKEN ROAST

INGREDIENTS

Chicken, cut into 4 pieces, make incisions on the pieces	750 gm
Ghee	¹/₂ cup / 100 gm / 3¹/₂ oz
For the marinade:	
Garlic (*lasan*) paste	1 tbsp / 12 gm
Yoghurt (*dahi*)	2 tbsp / 30 gm / 1 oz
Salt	1 tsp / 3 gm
Dry red chillies (*sookhi lal mirch*), coarsely crushed	¹/₄ cup

METHOD

For the marinade, mix all the ingredients together and rub onto the chicken pieces. Refrigerate for about one hour.

Heat the ghee in a heavy-bottomed pan; add the chicken along with the marinade and cook on low heat until done. Then brown on high heat, sprinkling a little water so that a light gravy is formed.

Serve hot with mint chutney and nan.

The Darra e Khyber, to call it (Khyber Pass) by its proper name, is not in fact a specific point but a narrow, vulnerable passage running through the Suleiman mountains. At the narrowest point it, till broadened, was just 3 m wide allowing barely two laden camels to pass. The British engineer Victor Belay had proposed laying a rail track along this route as early as 1880 but despite the strategic significance the line could not be laid till 1925. Marauding tribesmen looted passing trains and claimed unfettered right of free travel and the section soon fell into disrepair. The upstart challenger to the historic highway was, some said, put in its place.

MURGH BOTI

SERVES: 4

CHICKEN BAR-BE-QUE

INGREDIENTS

Chicken, cut into 8 pieces	750 gm / 26 oz
Garlic (*lasan*) paste	1 tbsp / 18 gm
Red chilli powder	1 tsp / 3 gm
Salt	1 tsp / 3 gm
Chaat masala	1 tsp / 3 gm
Ginger (*adrak*) paste	1 tsp / 6 gm
Yoghurt (*dahi*)	2 tbsp / 30 gm / 1 oz
Juice of lemon (*nimbu*)	1
Butter	¼ cup / 50 gm / 1¾ oz

METHOD

Mix all the ingredients together and marinate the chicken in this mixture for 2 hours. Refrigerate.

Preheat the oven at 180°C / 350°F. Brush the chicken with butter and grill in the oven for 15 minutes. Remove from the oven, turn the pieces over and put it back. Bake for another 15 minutes or until the chicken is done. Alternatively, the chicken can be skewered and barbequed on charcoal

Serve with chutney and nan.

MURGH KARI

SERVES: 4

CHICKEN CURRY

INGREDIENTS

Chicken, cut into 8 pieces	750 gm / 26 oz
Garlic (*lasan*) paste	1 tbsp / 18 gm
Ginger (*adrak*) paste	1 tbsp / 18 gm
Salt	1 tsp / 3 gm
Red chilli powder	1 tsp / 3 gm
Vegetable oil	3 tbsp / 45 ml / 1½ fl oz
Tomatoes, chopped	500 gm / 1.1 lb
Green chillies, chopped	5-6
Coriander (*dhaniya*) seeds	1 tsp / 2 gm

METHOD

Cook the chicken in a wok (*kadhai*). Add garlic paste, ginger paste, salt, red chilli powder, and oil. Reduce heat and cook for about 15 minutes or until the chicken is tender. Increase heat and cook for 5 minutes more or until the juice evaporates and the oil separates.

Add tomatoes, green chillies and coriander seeds. Cook for 5-10 minutes or until the water from the mixture evaporates.

Serve hot with nan or roti.

If you strain your eyes you can perhaps trace the Durand Line marking the divide between British India and Afghanistan. This is verily a no man's land—only the strongest survive in this region—flooded with drugs and guns. Darra Adam Khel, the village of the Adam clan, is famous for its home-made working replicas of any gun that is shown to the gifted gunsmiths here. This unusual skill was acquired when the British set up an arms factory here in 1897. They turned a blind eye to illicit arms manufacture in exchange of the Pathans not looting British arms and not molesting wayfarers on the road from Peshawar to Kohat.

Facing page: Khyber Pass

SHALGAM GOSHT

Food Path: Cuisine along the Grand Trunk Road

LAMB COOKED WITH TURNIPS

INGREDIENTS

Lamb	500 gm / 1.1 lb
Turnips (*shalgam*), peeled, quartered	1 kg / 2.2 lb
Turmeric (*haldi*) powder	1 tsp / 3 gm
Salt	1 tsp / 3 gm
Vegetable oil for frying	
Vegetable oil	2 tbsp / 30 ml / 1 fl oz
Onions, medium-sized, chopped	2-3
Garlic (*lasan*) paste	1 tsp / 6 gm
Tomatoes, medium-sized chopped	2-3
Red chilli powder	1 tsp / 3 gm
Coriander (*dhaniya*) powder	1 tsp / 3 gm
Green chillies, chopped for garnishing	
Green coriander (*hara dhaniya*), chopped for garnishing	

METHOD

Prick the turnips with a fork. Rub turmeric powder and salt all over the turnips. Keep aside for an hour.

Then wipe the turnips thoroughly with a paper towel.

Heat the oil in a frying pan; fry the turnips until golden brown. Remove and drain the excess oil on absorbent paper towels.

Heat the oil in a pot; add the onions and sauté till slightly brown. Add garlic paste, tomatoes, the spices, and the lamb; sauté till the lamb turns brown. Add 1 cup of water and cook on low heat until the meat is tender and a thick gravy is left.

Add the fried turnips and stir well. Remove and serve garnished with green chillies and green coriander and accompanied with nan.

Peshawar is the quintessential frontier outpost—landing stage and watering hole for caravans for centuries. Although a massive influx of refugees from Afghanistan, in recent years, has transformed it almost beyond recognition, it continues to pulsate with suppressed yet infectious excitement. The traveller on the GT Road can include in the sightseeing itinerary the Bala Hisar Fort, originally built by Babur, the founder of the Mughal dynasty (1526-1530), which dominates the eastern and western approaches to the city with its huge ramparts and embattlements.

Bala Hisar Fort

SAFED GOSHT

STEWED LAMB

INGREDIENTS

Lamb with lard (*charbi*)	1 kg / 2.2 lb
Lamb lard	250 gm / 9 oz
Garlic (*lasan*) paste	2 tsp / 12 gm
Salt	1 tsp / 3 gm
Coriander (*dhaniya*) powder	1 tsp / 3 gm
Water	2-3 cups / 500-750 ml / 16-24 fl oz

METHOD

Cook the lard in a pot (*handi*) on high heat until it melts. Add lamb and garlic paste; cook until light golden.

Add salt and coriander powder; stir-fry for a minute.

Add water and simmer for an hour or until the meat is tender. Cook on high heat until the gravy thickens.

Serve hot with lemon wedges.

PASANDE

SPICY LAMB STEAKS COOKED IN YOGHURT

INGREDIENTS

Lamb, boneless steaks (*pasande*)	500 gm / 1.1 lb
Vegetable oil	2 tbsp / 30 ml / 1 fl oz
Onions, cut into rings	1 cup / 120 gm / 4 oz
Garlic (*lasan*)	1
Green cardamom (*choti elaichi*), powdered	10
Yoghurt (*dahi*)	1 cup / 250 gm / 8 oz
Garam masala powder	1 tbsp / 9 gm
Turmeric (*haldi*) powder	¹/₂ tsp / 1¹/₂ gm
Red chilli powder	1 tsp / 3 gm
Coriander (*dhaniya*) powder	1 tsp / 3 gm
Green coriander (*hara dhaniya*), chopped for garnishing	

METHOD

Heat the oil in a pan; fry the onions till golden brown. Add the meat and fry on low heat till brown.

Add garlic, green cardamom, and a dash of water; stir-fry for a while. Add yoghurt and stir again. When water from the yoghurt evaporates, add all the spices and mix well. Add 1 cup of water and cook till the meat is tender and the oil separates.

Remove and transfer to a dish. Serve garnished with green coriander.

The Bala Hisar Fort was repaired and largely rebuilt by the Sikh military governor of the province during the reign of Maharaja Ranjit Singh, who had employed French engineers for this task. The museum here boasts of a collection of Gandhara statues unmatched elsewhere in the world. The Qissa Khawani Bazaar, the street of storytellers, runs east to west in the heart of the city where professionals used to regale weary travellers with tales of love and war. It makes a valiant effort to retain an aura of conspiratorial gossiping though it is becoming increasingly difficult to spot traditionally-clad camel drivers.

KADHAI NAMAK MANDI

SERVES: 4-6

LAMB CUBES TOSSED WITH TOMATOES AND GINGER

INGREDIENTS

Lamb, cut into pieces	850 gm / 30 oz
Lard	150 gm / 5 oz
Salt	1 tsp / 3 gm
Tomatoes, medium-sized, chopped	4-5
Green chillies, chopped	4-5
Ginger (adrak), finely chopped	1 tsp / 3 gm
Garlic (lasan) paste	1 tsp / 6 gm

METHOD

Take the lamb and lard in a wok (kadhai); add salt and cook covered on low heat for 20-25 minutes. Open the lid turn over the lamb and brown till the water evaporates and ghee floats on the surface.

Add tomatoes, green chillies, ginger, and garlic; stir for a few minutes,

Serve hot with nan.

NAMAK MANDI TIKKA

SERVES: 4-6

SKEWERED LAMB CUBES

INGREDIENTS

| Lamb, cut into medium-sized pieces | 1 kg / 2.2 lb |
| Salt | 1 tsp / 3 gm |

METHOD

Skewer the lamb and sprinkle salt over it. Cook on medium-hot coal for about 20-25 minutes, turning after every 45 seconds, till the meat is tender.

Note: This is the oldest method of making tikka in Peshawar and is very famous all over the country. It is a very delicious dish. Peshawar's *namak mandi* is actually a bazaar famous for lamb tikka and *kadhai*.

Bazaar Bataer Bazan, literally the street of partridge lovers, used to be a quaint tourist attraction but has changed beyond recognition in recent years. It is full of curio shops and the birds shops seem to have all disappeared. A major landmark is the beautiful Masjid Mahabat Khan, the mosque built by Mahabat Khan, governor of this province during the reign of Shah Jahan (1628-1658). The minarets, we are told at times, doubled as gallows to mete out exemplary punishment to rebels. Must pick souvenirs are the sturdy and stylish Peshawari sandals and Karakuli fur caps.

The spread of Islam to this region, starting in the eighth century, has given a basic character to the food of the people. Lamb, beef, chicken, and fish are the main foods.

MASALEDAAR BAINGAN

SERVES: 4

SPICED AUBERGINES

INGREDIENTS

Aubergines (*baingan*), large, washed, cut into rounds	500 gm / 1.1 lb
Salt	1 tsp / 3 gm
Onions, finely chopped	2
Garlic (*lasan*), finely chopped	1 tsp / 3 gm
Green chillies, finely chopped	2
Sugar	½ tsp
Vinegar (*sirka*)	4 tsp / 20 ml
Vegetable oil	2 tbsp / 30 ml / 1 fl oz
Turmeric (*haldi*) powder	½ tsp / 1½ gm
Ginger powder (*sonth*)	1 tsp / 3 gm
Yoghurt (*dahi*)	½ cup / 120 gm / 4 oz

METHOD

Sprinkle salt over the aubergines and keep aside for 10 minutes.

Wash with cold water.

Mix onions, garlic, and green chillies together.

Mix sugar and vinegar.

Heat the oil in a pan; fry the aubergines till brown. Add the other ingredients and cook for 10-15 minutes. Serve hot.

GANDANA KA SAAG

SERVES: 4

SPINACH COOKED WITH GARLIC

INGREDIENTS

Local spinach (*gandana*), finely chopped, boiled	4 cups
Vegetable oil	2 tbsp / 30 ml / 1 fl oz
Garlic (*lasan*) paste	2 tbsp / 24 gm
Dry red chillies (*sookhi lal mirch*), coarsely pounded	2 tsp / 4 gm
Salt	1 tsp / 3 gm

METHOD

Heat the oil in a pan; add garlic paste and sauté till it is about to change colour.

Add powdered dry red chillies, salt, and 1 tbsp water; mix well.

Add the spinach and cook until the water has evaporated and the oil separates.

Some of the Muslim feasts have special celebratory dishes. Eid-ul-Adha, which commemorates the Prophet Ibrahim's readiness to obey God even to the point of being willing to sacrifice his son, is observed by the sacrifice of a goat, a lamb, or a cow from which special dishes are made.

On Eid-ul-Fitr, which marks the end of Ramadan, the month of fasting in the Islamic calendar, the serving of a special dessert of vermicelli cooked in milk is a must. Almond and pistachios are added as decorations as is the silver foil (*varq*).

Peshawari nan hot from the oven. *Facing page:* The master shoemaker showcasing traditional footwear.

KARHI

GRAM FLOUR FRITTERS IN YOGHURT CURRY

INGREDIENTS

For the gravy:

Gram flour (*besan*)	2 tbsp / 20 gm
Yoghurt (*dahi*)	2 cups / 500 gm / 1.1 lb
Turmeric (*haldi*) powder	2 tsp / 6 gm
Red pepper	1 tsp
Salt	1 tsp / 3 gm
Water	2 cups / 500 ml / 16 fl oz

For the dumplings (*pakora*):

Gram flour	1 cup / 100 gm / 3½ oz
Red pepper	1 tsp
Salt	1 tsp / 3 gm

Black cumin	
(*shahi jeera*) seeds	1 tsp / 2 gm
Baking soda	½ tsp
Onion, medium-sized, chopped	1
Water	½ cup / 125 ml / 4 fl oz
Vegetable oil for frying	

For the tempering (*tarka*):

Vegetable oil	2 tbsp / 30 ml / 1 fl oz
Cumin (*jeera*) seeds	1 tsp / 2 gm
Dry red chillies (*sookhi lal mirch*)	2-3

METHOD

For the gravy:

Take all the ingredients in a pan and mix in a blender. Cook on medium heat and keep stirring until the mixture comes to the boil. Reduce heat and simmer for 10 minutes. Remove and keep warm.

For the dumplings:

Mix all the ingredients (except oil) together and make a batter.

Heat the oil in frying pan; lower spoonful of batter and fry till golden brown. Remove and repeat till all the batter is used up. Add the dumplings to the yoghurt curry.

For the tempering:

Heat the oil in a frying pan; add the cumin seeds and dry red chillies; sauté for a few seconds. Add to the curry.

Another major influence in the development of this region's cuisine was the establishment of the Mughal Empire starting in 1526. The opulent tastes exhibited by such emperors as Humayun, Akbar, Jahangir, and Shah Jahan in art, architecture, music, dance, and jewellery were also extended to food.

A style of cooking called Mughlai evolved at the Mughal court and even today it remains centred in Lahore. Some latter-day and widely-known survivors of court cuisine are, for example, *murgh mussalam*, in which the entire chicken is roasted with special spices and ingredients. *Shahi Tukra* is another leftover from the days of the Mughals. Perhaps the zenith in Mughal cuisine was reached when the imperial chefs perfected the recipes for aromatic pulaos and melt-in-the-month kebabs.

CHICKPEAS AND RAISIN LAMB RICE

INGREDIENTS

Rice, soaked	3 cups / 600 gm / 22 oz	Black cumin		
Beef / lamb	1 kg / 2.2 lb	(shahi jeera) seeds	1 tsp / 2½ gm	
Garlic (lasan) paste	2 tsp / 12 gm	Black cardamom (moti elaichi)	3-4	
Coriander (dhaniya) powder	1 tsp / 3 gm	Salt to taste		
Vegetable oil	1 cup / 250 ml / 8 fl oz	Tomatoes, chopped	1-2	
Onions, chopped	2 cups / 250 gm / 9 oz	Chickpeas (kabuli chana),		
Black peppercorns		boiled	1 cup / 150 gm / 5 oz	
(sabut kaali mirch)	a few seeds	Raisins (kishmish)	1 cup / 170 gm / 6 oz	
Cinnamon (dalchini), 1" sticks	2	Garam masala powder	1 tsp / 3 gm	
Cloves (laung)	5-6	Ginger powder (sonth)	1 tsp / 3 gm	
Cumin (jeera) seeds	1 tsp / 2 gm			

METHOD

Cook the meat in a pot. Add garlic paste and coriander powder; sauté for a few minutes. Add 6-8 cups of water and bring the mixture to the boil. Reduce heat and simmer for about an hour or until the gravy is thick and the lamb is soft. Remove the lamb pieces and keep aside. Reserve the soup.

Heat the oil in a pot; add the onions and fry until dark brown. Remove the onions and keep aside. When cool grind the onions to a paste.

In the same pot add cooked lamb, whole garam masala, salt, and tomatoes. Cook until the lamb browns evenly.

Add the reserved 6 cups of soup and bring the mixture to the boil. Add ground onion paste and drained rice. When the rice is ³/₄th cooked add chickpeas and raisins. Reduce heat, add garam masala and ginger powders; cook for about 20-30 minutes or until rice is ready to serve.

Variations: **Narangi Pulau** (rice with orange rinds): Instead of chickpeas and raisins add fine strips of orange rinds previously boiled, drained and sautéed in little oil. Add 2 tsp sugar.

Cuisine in Pakistan has always had a regional character, with each of the four provinces offering special dishes. In the Punjab, for example, the Mughlai cuisine influence is prominent. In Baluchistan, cooks use the *sajji* method of barbecuing whole lambs and stick bread in a deep pit. Cooking in the North West Frontier Province is a great deal plainer and involves the heavy use of lamb.

Food in Peshawar is closer to Afghan fare than to the Punjabi repast. This is the place to sample the most succulent *barra* culled, according to legend, from the calf removed from the womb, and the *chappali* kebab, shaped like the city's famous footwear. Another unusual delicacy encountered coyly hiding behind a thin translucent veil of egg batter is the *bannu* kebab, an import from

ZARDA

SERVES: 4

MEETHAY CHAWAL

INGREDIENTS

Rice	2 cups / 400 gm / 14 oz
Orange food colour	1 tsp / 5 ml
Water	1½ cups / 375 ml / 6 fl oz
Ghee	½ cup / 125 gm / 4 oz
Green cardamom (*choti elaichi*)	6
Sugar	2 cups / 400 gm / 14 oz
Almonds / pistachios	
(*badaam / pista*) as desired, chopped	

METHOD

Mix the food colour with the water and bring to the boil. Add rice and cook until almost done. Remove and drain the rice in a colander.

Heat the ghee in a pot; add green cardamom, sugar, and 6 cups of water. Boil till the sugar dissolves completely. Add rice, stir and simmer on medium heat.

Serve hot garnished with almonds or pistachios.

GAJRELA

SERVES: 4

CARROT KHEER

INGREDIENTS

Carrots (*gajar*), shredded	500 gm / 1.1 lb
Milk	12 cups / 3 lt / 6 pints
Rice, washed, soaked, drained	¼ cup / 50 gm / 1¾ oz
Sugar	1 cup / 200 gm / 7 oz

METHOD

Boil the milk in a pan. Add carrots and rice and cook on medium heat. Do not stir.

When the liquid is of desired consistency, add sugar and cook for another 10 minutes. Remove and grind the mixture in a blender till it resembles the consistency of *kheer*. If desired add almonds

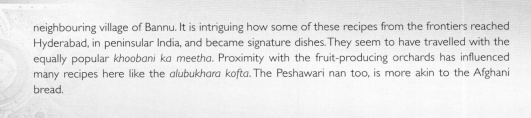

neighbouring village of Bannu. It is intriguing how some of these recipes from the frontiers reached Hyderabad, in peninsular India, and became signature dishes. They seem to have travelled with the equally popular *khoobani ka meetha*. Proximity with the fruit-producing orchards has influenced many recipes here like the *alubukhara kofta*. The Peshawari nan too, is more akin to the Afghani bread.

SHREDDED CARROTS WITH ALMONDS

INGREDIENTS

Carrots (gajar),	
washed, shredded	1 kg / 2.2 lb
Milk	8 cups / 2 lt / 4 pints
Sugar	1 cup / 200 gm / 7 oz
Vegetable oil	1 cup / 250 ml / 8 fl oz
Almonds (badaam),	
chopped	1 cup / 120 gm / 4 oz
Green cardamom	
(choti elaichi)	5-6

METHOD

Heat the milk in a pot. Add the carrots and bring to the boil. Reduce heat and simmer for 1 hour. Increase heat and let the milk evaporate. Add sugar and oil, stir and brown.

When the oil separates from the mixture, add almonds and green cardamom. Serve hot.

SEMOLINA PUDDING

INGREDIENTS

Semolina (suji),	
soaked in water	1 cup / 100 gm / 3½ oz
Vegetable oil	1 cup / 250 ml / 8 fl oz
Sugar	1 cup / 200 gm / 7 oz
Water	1 cup / 250 ml / 8 fl oz
Green cardamom (choti elaichi)	2-3
Pistachios (pista), chopped	2 tsp
Almonds (badaam), chopped	2 tsp

METHOD

Heat the oil in a cooking pan; add sugar and cook until it caramelizes. Add water and stir until well mixed.

Add semolina and stir constantly for about 15 minutes.

Add green cardamom and mix. Remove and serve hot garnished with pistachios and almonds.

Food Path: Cuisine along the Grand Trunk Road

ROASTED LEG OF LAMB

INGREDIENTS

Whole leg of lamb, fat trimmed	2¹/₂-3 kg / 5.5-6.6 lb
Lemon (nimbu) juice	4 tbsp / 60 ml / 2 fl oz
Garlic (lasan) paste	1 tbsp / 18 gm
Salt	3 tsp / 9 gm
Black pepper (kaali mirch)	2 tsp / 6 gm
Coriander (dhaniya) powder	1 tbsp / 9 gm
Nutmeg (jaiphal) powder	¹/₄ tsp
Cumin (jeera) powder	1 tbsp / 9 gm
Yoghurt (dahi)	1 cup / 250 gm / 9 oz
Vegetable oil	¹/₂ cup / 125 ml / 4 fl oz

METHOD

Prick the lamb thoroughly with a sharp knife or cut small slits all over the lamb with a sharp knife. Place the lamb in a deep baking dish, spread lemon juice all over and rub into the slits. Cover and refrigerate for an hour.

Combine garlic paste, salt, black pepper, coriander, nutmeg and cumin powders, and yoghurt in a small bowl; mix well.

Pour the marinade over the lamb and coat well all over. Cover and refrigerate again for 6-8 hours or preferably overnight.

Preheat the grill and grill the lamb on an oiled rack set for 10-15 minutes on each side. At the end of cooking time baste with oil.

Serve hot with nan and chutney of your choice.

Rawalpindi or Pindi to its lovers is another fascinating city along the Grand Trunk Road. Close by lie the ruins of Taxila, an internationally renowned centre of academic excellence in the centuries before the birth of Christ. This was a city Alexander the Great passed through on his way to the Indian heartland.

Subsequently, the area came under the sway of the Kushan dynasty and is one of the richest repositories of Indo-Greek Buddhist art. The hill station of Muree is within visiting distance. Truck painting garage-studios abound in Pindi and are as much of a tourist draw as the bustling Raja Bazaar and the Army Museum.

SPICY LAMB CHOPS

INGREDIENTS

Lamb chops, washed	1 kg / 2.2 lb	Carom seeds (*ajwain*),	
Salt	1 tsp / 3 gm	powdered	a pinch
Ground to a paste:			
Green chillies	6	Yoghurt (*dahi*)	1 cup / 250 gm / 9 oz
Green coriander		Garlic (*lasan*) paste	1 tsp / 6 gm
(*hara dhaniya*), chopped	a few leaves	Ginger (*adrak*) paste	2 tsp / 12 gm
Mint (*pudina*) leaves	a few leaves	Ghee	½ cup / 125 gm / 4 oz
Black peppercorns		Onions, medium-sized, chopped	2
(*sabut kaali mirch*)	10	Potato, boiled, cubed	1
Cloves (*laung*)	2	Green peas (*hara mattar*),	
Green cardamom (*choti elaichi*)	3-4	boiled	1 cup

METHOD

Sprinkle the lamb chops with salt and leave aside for a few minutes.

Mix the ground paste with the yoghurt. Add garlic and ginger paste. Marinate the chops in this mixture for 1 hour.

Heat the ghee in a pot; add onions and sauté till golden brown. Remove the onions from the ghee, chop into fine pieces and mix with lamb mixture.

In the same ghee add the lamb mixture and cook on low heat for 30 minutes till tender. Increase heat and roast the lamb till the yoghurt water is dried and thick gravy is left.

Serve hot garnished with boiled potato and green peas.

The cooks from Pindi along with those from Peshawar are the ones who have gifted to the world a tandoori and *balti* delicacies. *Pindi chana* is arguably on top of the heap in the *choley* genre. Pair it with *kulche / bhature* and you have a balanced meal—an unalloyed delight for the prince and pauper alike.

Rawalpindi served for a short period as Pakistan's capital. This honour now belongs to its twin city Islamabad, designed by a Dutch urban planner and settled symmetrically along the grids.

Rawalpindi Railway Station

Street Foods of Pakistan

Lahore is the gourmet capital of Pakistan and the 'pit stop' threatens to degenerate into a glutton's splurge unless one is constantly on guard. There are many outstanding eateries and it is difficult to single out any. Bundu Khan finds favour with most foodie opinion polls. The food is predominantly non-vegetarian, biased in favour of the tandoor, akin to, yet tantalizingly different from, the fare served on the eastern side of the Wagah border.

Rawalpindi, Pindi to those smitten by the city, is where the transition to North West Frontier Province cuisine is perceptible. The Afghani preference for lamb and chargrilled kebab is distinctly noticeable. Jahangir Balti is famous for his *murgh kadhai* and succulent tikka. The *kadhai* speciality is very different from the dishes sharing the name elsewhere. Anwar Cafi, situated opposite the mosque, has its own loyal patrons who swear by its *murgh* biryani, *murgh qorma,* and *raita*.

Peshawar is a historic city renowned even before the birth of Christ. This is where the tribal world begins and preparations were made for the passage across the Khyber Pass. It used to be the quintessential frontier town marking the Imperial divide, full of romance, till the large-scale influx of refugees from Afghanistan and blurring of the borders changed it.

Qissa Khawani Bazaar may no longer be crowded by camel caravans, but it continues to be abuzz with locals and tourists drawn by the street snacks. But if you take food seriously you must head for the Khyber Bazaar lined with dozens of kebab shops. The local favourites are the *chappali kebab* (a fatty lamb mince patty shaped like the sandal that takes its name after the city). Surprisingly, excellent Bengali sweets like *rosogolla* and *rasmalai* are available at Nirala Sweets which compete with the myriad kebabs here.

The *tawa* artist preparing a *taka-tin* delicacy. *Facing page:* Grills and roasts are the most popular fare at the roadside stalls. Deep-fried sweets tickle the sweet tooth.

MEAT COOKED WITH MIXED DALS AND GROUNDED WHEAT

INGREDIENTS

Beef / Lamb, boneless	2 kg / 4.4 lb
Bengal gram (*chana dal*), washed,	
soaked for 1 hour	1 cup / 200 gm / 7 oz
Lentil (*masoor dal*), washed,	
soaked for 1 hour	1 cup / 200 gm / 7 oz
Green gram (*moong*), washed,	
soaked for 1 hour	1 cup / 200 gm / 7 oz
Black gram (*urad*), washed,	
soaked for 1 hour	1 cup / 200 gm / 7 oz
Rice	1 cup / 200 gm / 7 oz
Vegetable oil	3 cups / 750 ml / 24 fl oz
Onions, chopped	2 cups / 250 gm / 9 oz
Garlic (*lasan*) paste	2 tsp / 12 gm
Tomatoes, chopped	250 gm / 9 oz
Salt	3 tsp / 9 gm
Red chilli powder	3 tsp / 9 gm
Turmeric (*haldi*) powder	1 tsp / 3 gm
Grounded wheat (*dalia*)	1 cup
Garam masala powder	3 tsp / 9 gm
Chaat masala	2 tsp / 6 gm
Ginger (*adrak*),	
thinly sliced	100 gm / 3½ oz
Green chillies, sliced	25 gm
Lemon (*nimbu*)	2

METHOD

Boil the Bengal gram with 1 tsp of salt and 8 cups water for 20 minutes. Add the other dals and rice; bring to the boil. Reduce heat and simmer for about 1 hour or till cooked. Stir the mixture vigorously enough to mash it or blend it in a blender. Keep warm.

Heat 1 cup of oil; add the onions and sauté till golden. Add garlic paste, stir and add meat, tomatoes, salt, red chilli and turmeric powders; stir for another minute. Add 2 cups of water bring to the boil then let it simmer for 1 hour or till the meat is tender. Increase heat and brown the meat until the water is completely evaporated and a thick gravy remains. Remove and grind the meat and mix with the gravy. In another pan boil the grounded wheat with 1 tsp of salt and 2 cups of water until tender. Mix the dal mixture with the meat mixture and ground wheat stirring constantly, reduce heat and add garam masala and *chaat* masala.

Heat the remaining oil; add 1 chopped onion and sauté till brown. Add ginger; mix and remove. Pour the oil into the *haleem* and serve hot garnished with green coriander, lemon, ginger, and green chillies.

Pindi immediately brings to mind Chandigarh in India, brainchild of the French architect Le Corbousier. The local Pakistanis feel that both Pindi and Islamabad are bursting at the seams and the sprawling settlements in these cities are soon going to merge and mock the man-made divide. It is difficult to imagine though how this is going to bridge the psychological distance that separates the historic old from the pretentious new.

ALOO GOSHT

LAMB COOKED WITH POTATOES—LAHORI STYLE

INGREDIENTS

Lamb / Beef	1 kg / 2.2 lb
Potatoes, medium-sized,	
peeled, cut into 2 pieces	250 gm / 9 oz
Vegetable oil	1 cup/ 250 ml / 4 fl oz
Onions, medium-sized	4
Ginger-garlic	
(adrak-lasan) paste	1 tbsp / 18 gm
Green cardamom	
(choti elaichi), powdered	4-5
Dry fenugreek leaf	
(kasoori methi) powder	1 tbsp / 1½ gm
Tomatoes, medium-sized	3-4
Yoghurt (dahi)	1 tbsp / 15 gm
Salt	1 tsp / 3 gm

Red chilli powder	1 tsp / 3 gm
Turmeric (haldi) powder	½ tsp / 1½ gm
Coriander (dhaniya) powder	1 tsp / 3 gm
Water	3 cups / 750 ml / 24 fl oz
Black cumin (shahi jeera)	
seeds	1 tsp / 2½ gm
Black peppercorns	
(sabut kaali mirch)	8
Cloves (laung)	4
Cinnamon (dalchini), 1" stick	1
Green coriander	
(hara dhaniya), chopped	½ cup / 25 gm
Green chillies, chopped for garnishing	

METHOD

Heat the oil in a heavy-bottomed pan: add onions and sauté till golden brown. Add ginger-garlic paste and cook for 1 minute. Add green cardamom, dry fenugreek leaf powder, and tomatoes; cook for 2-3 minutes.

Add yoghurt, salt, red chilli, turmeric and coriander powders; stirring continuously on high heat till the oil separates. Add meat and stir-fry on high heat till the meat changes colour and spices coat the meat. Add about 2 cups of water, when the water boils turn the heat to low and let it simmer for about half an hour or till the meat

is tender. Increase the heat to high till the water evaporates. Add the potatoes and stir-fry on high heat for about 2-3 minutes or till they are well coated with the spices.

Powder black cumin seeds, black peppercorns, cloves, and cinnamon and add to the potato mixture. Add 1½ cups of water, let it simmer until the potatoes are tender and a thick gravy is left.

Serve hot garnished with green coriander and green chillies, and accompanied with rice or chapattis.

MACHCHI KE KEBAB

FISH KEBABS

INGREDIENTS

Fish (singhara)	500 gm / 1.1 lb	Cottage cheese (*paneer*),		
Salt	1 tsp / 3 gm	chopped	125 gm / 4 oz
Red chilli powder	1 tsp / 3 gm	Eggs, beaten	2
Garam masala powder	1 tsp / 3 gm	Breadcrumbs	1 cup / 120 gm / 4 oz
Cumin (*jeera*) seeds	1 tsp / 2 gm	Vegetable oil for frying	
Onions, chopped	1 cup / 125 gm / 4 oz		
Garlic (*lasan*), chopped	2 tsp / 6 gm		
Ginger (*adrak*), chopped	125 gm / 4 oz		
Green coriander			
(*hara dhaniya*), chopped	a few leaves		
Green chillies, chopped	2-3		

METHOD

Rub salt over the fish and keep aside for 10 minutes. Wash.

In a pan mix the fish, red chilli and garam masala powders, and cumin seeds together. Add onions, garlic, ginger, and 1 cup of water. Bring the mixture to the boil. Cook for 20 minutes. Remove from heat, and keep aside to cool.

Remove the fish bones and add green coriander, green chillies, and cottage cheese; mix well. Divide the mixture equally and shape each into a round kebab. Dip each kebab in egg and then roll over the breadcrumbs.

Heat the oil in a frying pan; add the kebabs, one at a time, and brown both sides. Remove with a slotted spoon and drain the excess oil.

Serve hot garnished with French fries and accompanied with tomato sauce.

Lahore, a city that traces its origins to the mythological times, named after a son of Ram, the prince of Ayodhya and hero of the Hindu epic the *Ramayan*, once famed as the Paris of the Orient, lost much of its old luster after Partition and the building of the new capital Islamabad. It remains without doubt the Mecca for the gourmet. Many of the historic buildings, the Shahi Fort, the Nishat Bagh and the Moti Masjid for instance remind the onlooker of their twins in India. The mausoleum of Jahangir and his wife Noor Jahan's tomb too attract a lot of visitors.

Facing page: Grilling on open fire seems to be more popular in Pakistan than baking in a tandoor.

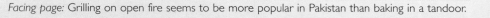

FISH AND POTATO CURRY

INGREDIENTS

Fish	500 gm / 1.1 lb	Green chillies, chopped		2-3
Salt	1 tsp / 3 gm	Green coriander		
Garlic (*lasan*) paste	½ cup	(*hara dhaniya*), chopped		2 tbsp / 8 gm
Red chilli powder	1 tsp / 3 gm			
Lemon (*nimbu*) juice	2 tbsp / 30 ml / 1 fl oz			
Vegetable oil for frying the fish				
Vegetable oil	2 tbsp / 30 ml / 1 fl oz			
Ginger (*adrak*) paste	1 tbsp / 18 gm			
Turmeric (*haldi*) powder	1 tsp / 3 gm			
Coriander (*dhaniya*) powder	1 tsp / 3 gm			
Yoghurt (*dahi*)	1 cup / 250 gm / 9 oz			
Potatoes, cut diagonally	250 gm / 9 oz			
Dry fenugreek leaf				
(*kasoori methi*) powder	2 tbsp / 3 gm			

METHOD

Rub salt over the fish and keep aside for 10 minutes. Wash.

Mix 1 tsp garlic paste, 1 tsp salt, red chilli powder, and lemon juice together. Marinate the fish in this mixture for half an hour.

Heat the oil for frying in a pan; add the fish pieces and brown on both sides. Remove and keep warm.

Heat 2 tbsp oil in a pan; add the remaining garlic and ginger pastes; sauté till the colour changes. Add turmeric and coriander powders; stir for a few seconds. Add the yoghurt and mix well. Add potatoes and stir for 5 minutes. Add 1 cup of water and simmer for 20 minutes. Add fish pieces, lower heat and cook covered for 10 minutes. Remove. Garnish with dry fenugreek leaf powder, green chilies, and green coriander.

Serve hot with steamed rice or tandoori nan.

TALLI MACHCHI

SERVES: 4

FRIED FISH

INGREDIENTS

Fish	500 gm / 1.1 lb
Garlic (lasan) paste	2 tbsp / 26 gm
Salt	1 tsp / 3 gm
Red chilli powder	1 tsp / 3 gm
Cumin (jeera) seeds	1 tsp / 2 gm
Coriander (dhaniya) powder	1 tsp / 3 gm
Carom (ajwain) seeds	1 tsp / 2½ gm
White vinegar (sirka)	1 tbsp / 15 ml
Lemon (nimbu) juice	2 tbsp / 30 ml / 1 fl oz
Gram flour (besan)	2 tbsp / 20 gm
Vegetable oil for frying	

METHOD

Sprinkle salt on the fish and leave aside for 10 minutes. Wash.

Mix all the ingredients except oil and marinate the fish in the mixture. Cover and leave aside for an hour in the refrigerator.

Heat the oil in a deep-frying pan; add the fish, one at a time, and fry on medium heat, till golden brown.

Serve with *dhaniye ki chutney*.

Lahore is the second most populous city in Pakistan and continues to be the most charming. It has many beautiful historic monuments testifying to its pre-eminence during the Mughal period. It is a city of myriad moods and great contrasts. In days gone by, Lahore, like Old Delhi, was enclosed by a massive 9 m high protective wall with thirteen gates merging into the natural moat provided by River Ravi, but the bustling population has since spilled much beyond its confines.

Facing page: Chai khanas are the subcontinent's version of a tea house or a cafe.

TORI ANDAY

SERVES: 4-6

RIDGE GOURDS WITH EGGS

INGREDIENTS

Ridge gourds (tori)	2 kg / 4.4 lb
Vegetable oil	2 tbsp / 30 ml / 1 fl oz
Onions, chopped	2 cups / 250 gm / 9 oz
Black pepper (kaali mirch)	1 tsp / 3 gm
Salt	1 tsp / 3 gm
For the omelet:	
Eggs, medium-sized	2
Capsicum (Shimla mirch), chopped	2-3
Onion, finely chopped	½
Cumin (jeera) seeds	¼ tsp
Salt	¼ tsp

METHOD

Heat the oil in a pan; add the onions and sauté until light golden. Add black pepper, ridge gourd, and salt. Stir and cook on low heat until the vegetable is tender. Reduce heat and cook until the water evaporates.

For the omelet: Mix all the ingredients together add the mixture to a frying pan greased with a little oil. Cook till the underside is lightly brown. Flip the omelet and cook the other side too. Remove and cut the omelet into small pieces.

Transfer the vegetable in a dish and mix the omelet. Serve garnished with green coriander.

BHARREY KARELEY

STUFFED BITTER GOURDS

INGREDIENTS

Bitter gourds (*karela*), large	1 kg / 2.2 lb	Red pepper	1 tsp
Salt	1 tsp / 3 gm	Ginger (*adrak*), finely chopped	1 tsp / 6 gm
For the stuffing:		Garam masala powder	1 tsp / 3 gm
Lamb, minced (*keema*)	500 gm / 1.1 lb	Coriander (*dhaniya*) powder	1 tsp / 3 gm
Onions, chopped	3-4	Cumin (*jeera*) seeds	1 tsp / 2 gm
Tomatoes, finely chopped	250 gm / 9 oz	Pomegranate seeds	
Green coriander		(*anaar dana*)	1 tsp / 3 gm
(*hara dhaniya*), fresh,			
finely chopped	2 tbsp / 8 gm	Vegetable oil for frying	
Capsicum (*Shimla mirch*),			
finely chopped	1-2		

METHOD

Peel the bitter gourds and sprinkle with salt. Keep aside for an hour.

Slit the bitter gourds lengthwise and deseed. Wash them in plenty of water. Drain out the water by squeezing them a little.

For the stuffing:
Grind the minced meat and onions in a chopper till smooth.

Mix the tomatoes, green coriander, capsicum, and red pepper with the remaining ingredients.

Mix the tomato mixture with the minced meat and fill the bitter gourds with this mixture. To seal the filling inside tie the bitter gourd with a thread. Repeat till all are done.

Heat the oil in the pan; fry the stuffed bitter gourds on very low heat (it should take at least an hour). The lower the flame and more slowly you fry the less bitter they are. When golden turn them onto a dish.

In the same pan, cook the remaining stuffing on low heat. Remove. Arrange all the bitter gourds around the stuffing on a platter and serve hot.

The city is full of beautiful mosques, many contend that the Wazir Khan Mosque in Kashmir Bazaar, decorated with tiles and Arabesque paintings, is the most beautiful in all of South Asia. Equally impressive is the Badshahi Mosque built by Emperor Aurengzeb and constructed of red sandstone at the Alamgiri Gate of the Lahore Fort. The 'samadhi of Maharaja Ranjit Singh' is a cenotaph that commemorates Maharaja Ranjit Singh, the founder of Khalsa rule in Punjab.

The Mall Road is a stately promenade curving gracefully for more than 5 km and has traditionally been the most fashionably modern part of the city.

SHALGAM KA BHARTA

SERVES: 4

MASHED TURNIPS

INGREDIENTS

Turnips (shalgam), washed, cut into 4 pieces	500 gm / 1.1 lb
Vegetable oil	4 tbsp / 60 ml / 2 fl oz
Onions, chopped	2 cups / 250 gm / 9 oz
Garlic (lasan) paste	1 tsp / 6 gm
Ginger (adrak) paste	1 tsp / 6 gm
Sesame (til) seeds	1 tsp / 3 gm
Cumin (jeera) seeds	1 tsp / 2 gm
Cloves (laung)	a few
Salt	1 tsp / 3 gm
Red chilli powder	1 tsp / 3 gm
Turmeric (haldi) powder	1 tsp / 3 gm
Yoghurt (dahi)	1 cup / 250 gm / 9 oz
Green coriander (hara dhaniya)	2 tsp / 8 gm
Green chillies	1-2
Garam masala powder	1 tsp / 3 gm

METHOD

Cook the turnips in a little water until tender. Remove and mash with a fork; keep warm.

Heat the oil in another pot; add the onions and cook till golden brown. Add garlic and ginger pastes, sesame seeds, cumin seeds, cloves, salt, red chilli and turmeric powders; stir for a minute.

Add yoghurt; mix and stir and add mashed turnips. Cook till the mixture is dry and the oil separates. Remove and serve garnished with green coriander, green chillies, and garam masala. Serve hot with nan.

KHATTI DAL

SERVES: 4

TANGY LENTIL

INGREDIENTS

Lentil (masoor) or split green gram (moong)	1 cup / 200 gm / 7 oz
Salt to taste	
Turmeric (haldi) powder	1 tsp / 3 gm
Ginger (adrak) paste	2 tsp / 12 gm
Lemon (nimbu) juice	2 tbsp / 30 ml / 1 fl oz
Sugar	1 tsp / 3 gm
Green chillies	2-3
Vegetable oil / Ghee	4 tbsp / 60 ml / 2 fl oz
Cumin (jeera) seeds	1/2 tsp / 1 gm

METHOD

Wash the dal and cook in 4 cups of water. Add salt and turmeric powder. Bring to the boil. Reduce heat and simmer gently till the dal is tender and cooked. Mix thoroughly till the mixture is like thick soup.

Add ginger paste, lemon juice, and sugar; cook for 2-3 minutes. Add green chillies.

Heat the oil / ghee in a frying pan; add the cumin seeds and sauté till they start popping. Remove and add to the dal.

BEEF COOKED WITH GREEN GRAM

INGREDIENTS

Beef, boneless	1 kg / 2.2 lb
Vegetable oil	3-4 cups / 750 ml-1 lt / 24-32 fl oz
Onions, chopped	2 cups / 250 gm / 9 oz
Garlic (*lasan*) paste	2 tsp / 12 gm
Salt	2½ tsp / 4½ gm
Black pepper (*kaali mirch*) powder	3-4 tsp / 9-12 gm
Broken wheat (*gandam / dalia*) soaked in water	1 cup
Rice	1¼ cups / 250 gm / 9 oz
Green gram (*sabut moong dal*)	1¼ cups / 250 gm / 9 oz
Ginger (*adrak*), cut into juliennes	50 gm / 1¾ oz

METHOD

Heat 1 cup of oil in a pan; add 1 chopped onion and sauté till golden. Add beef and garlic paste. When the beef turns light brown, add 4 cups of water, salt, and black pepper. Simmer for 1 hour or till the meat is tender. Take the meat out of the soup and grind it coarsely. Return to the soup; add broken wheat.

Boil the rice and green gram together in a pot until tender. Remove and add to the soup and meat mixture. Cook till the broken wheat is tender. If the mixture feels dry add just enough water so that it coats the spoon smoothly. Keep stirring until the mixture looks like a paste.

Heat the remaining oil in the pan; add the remaining chopped onions and sauté till golden brown. Remove and add to the soup mixture; mix well.

Serve hot garnished with brown onion and ginger.

NIHARI

BEEF STEW FLAVOURED WITH SPICES

INGREDIENTS

Beef	1 kg / 2.2 lb
Vegetable oil	1 cup / 250 ml / 4 fl oz
Onions, finely chopped	1 cup / 120 gm / 4 oz
Ginger (adrak) paste	3 tsp / 18 gm
Garlic (lasan) paste	3 tsp / 18 gm
Red chilli powder	1 tsp / 3 gm
Turmeric (haldi) powder	1 tsp / 3 gm
Coriander (dhaniya) powder	1 tsp / 3 gm
Salt	1 tsp / 3 gm
Bay leaves (tej patta)	2
Cloves (laung), powdered	4-5
Cinnamon (dalchini), 1" sticks, powdered	2-3
Aniseed (saunf), powdered	1 tsp / 2 gm
Green cardamom (choti elaichi)	4-5
Wholewheat flour (atta)	1 cup / 150 gm / 5 oz
Yoghurt (dahi)	2/3 cup / 160 gm / 5¼ oz
Mace (javitri), powdered	1 tsp / 3 gm
Green coriander (hara dhaniya), chopped for garnishing	

METHOD

Heat ½ cup oil in a pan; add onions and sauté for a while. Add meat and stir-fry till golden brown. Add ginger-garlic paste and cook on high heat. Add red chilli, turmeric and coriander powders, salt, and bay leaves; stir for about 1 minute.

Add about 6-8 cups of water and bring the mixture to the boil. Reduce heat and simmer for 1 hour. When the meat is tender take it out of the soup. Add powdered cloves, cinnamon, aniseed, and green cardamom; mix well.

Heat the remaining oil in a pan; add the wholewheat flour and stir for 1 minute. Add soup and yoghurt, stir constantly until the mixture thickens. Add meat and sprinkle mace powder, cover the pan and keep hot on low heat for 5 minutes. Serve hot garnished with green coriander

Gawalmandi is the famous food mall tempting the visitors and residents alike with irresistible delicacies. One can gorge on Mughlai, Punjabi, Afghani, Balti classics not to forget the hybrid innovations. Barbeque items are the most popular but it is the curries that draw the gourmet. The atmosphere is an integral part of dining here. Most of the buildings in this area date back to pre-Partition days and evoke strong nostalgia.

Anarkali Bazaar, named after the legendary courtesan in Emperor Akbar's court, who had bewitched Prince Salim, is arguably the most famous of the city's many bazaars. Its congested lanes

BEEF IN YOGHURT CURRY

INGREDIENTS

Paye (barey), cut into pieces	2 pieces	Tomato, medium-sized, chopped	1
Beef	1 kg / 2.2 lb	Yoghurt (dahi), whipped	1 cup / 250 gm / 9 oz
Salt	2 tsp / 6 gm	Garam masala powder	3 tsp / 9 gm
Red chilli powder	2 tsp / 6 gm	Green coriander (hara dhaniya)	1/2 cup / 25 gm
Garlic paste	2 tbsp / 36 gm / 1 1/4 oz	Green chillies, chopped	5-6
Onions, medium-sized, chopped	1-2	Lemon (nimbu), cut into wedges for garnishing	
Vegetable oil	2 tbsp / 30 ml / 1 fl oz		
Garlic (lasan) paste	1 tsp / 6 gm		
Ginger (adrak) paste	1 tsp / 6 gm		
Red chilli powder	1 tsp / 3 gm		

METHOD

Take the *paye* in a pan with 8 cups of water. Add salt, red chilli powder, garlic paste, and onions; boil for 1 hour on medium heat. Add beef and cook for another hour or till the *paye* and beef are tender and about 2-3 cups of soup is left.

Heat the oil in a pan; add garlic-ginger paste and cook on medium heat till brown. Add red chilli powder and tomato; stir for another minute. Add *paye* and beef with 1 tbsp of soup; stir gradually. Add the remaining soup.

Mix the yoghurt with garam masala and add to the *paye* mixture. Cover the pot with a lid and cook on low heat (dum) for about 5 minutes. Serve hot garnished with green coriander, green chillies, and lemon wedges

CHICKEN COOKED IN YOGHURT

INGREDIENTS

Chicken, cut into pieces	I kg / 2.2 lb
Yoghurt (dahi)	½ cup / 100 gm / 3½ oz
Onion, roughly chopped	I
Garlic (lasan)	I tsp / 6 gm
Green coriander / Mint	
(hara dhaniya/pudina)	½ cup / 25 gm
Vegetable oil	2 tbsp / 30 ml / I fl oz
Turmeric (haldi) powder	I tsp / 3 gm
Garam masala powder	I½ tsp / 4½ gm
Red chilli powder	I tsp / 3 gm
Salt	I½ tsp / 4½ gm
Tomatoes, diced	2

METHOD

Blend the onion, garlic, green coriander / mint to a smooth paste.

Heat the oil in a pan; fry the mixture, stirring continuously. Add turmeric and garam masala and red chilli powders, and salt; sauté for a another minute. Stir in yoghurt and tomatoes and cook until the liquid dries up and the consistency of the mixture is that of a thick purée. Add chicken pieces and mix well so that they are coated on both sides. Reduce heat, cover the pan tightly and cook until the chicken is tender. If there is a lot of liquid left after the chicken is cooked uncover increase heat and let the extra water evaporate, stirring gently.

Serve garnished with green coriander and accompanied with rice or chapattis.

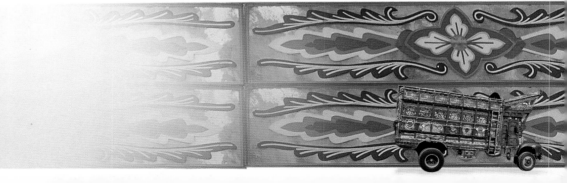

are full of small shops doing brisk business in traditional crafts like leatherwear, embroidered garments, glass bangles, beaten gold and silver jewellery, and silks.

One hundred and one kilometres west of Islamabad the travellers come across the historic Attock Fort. According to folklore the name derives from the Hindi-Urdu word *attok* that means an obstacle. Akbar had commanded his minister, Khwaza Shamsuddin, to construct it in the year

Facing page: Kites are not only child's play. The sport is taken seriously by many an adult.

The landscape may be a bit bleak and dusty but the quaint lorries—lovingly cared for well-preserved old beauties—and the sleek modern trucks plying the Pakistani stretch of the Grand Trunk Road try their best to break the tedium. They are painted all over—some favour shades of pastel turquoise, primrose pink and russet—reminding you of the delicate patterns woven in silken carpets or *jamawar* shawls, others mirror the minimalist abstract geometrical designs decorating white marble walls in a mosque or a palace. Most have no such aesthetic pretensions and are unabashedly kitsch—splashing bright blotches of colours—screaming scarlet, brilliant blue and garish green in a wayward manner.

This genre is very different from the body beautifying artwork in India. Islam prohibits depiction of human form and this eliminates replication of calendar

Truck Art
in Pakistan

or poster art. The Pakistani truck painters cope with the challenge most imaginatively by incorporating multi-hued flowers, pheasants and landscape. The effect is quite often spell-binding. The whole, as they say, is greater than the sum of its parts and some of these unusual canvases, framed in glittering chrome, look like a magnified Central Asian miniature or a page out of an illuminated manuscript recalling a body covered with seductive tattoos.

KHEER

RICE PUDDING

INGREDIENTS

Full-cream milk	16 cups / 4 lt / 8 pints
Rice, soaked in water	1 cup / 200 gm / 7 oz
Sugar	2 cups / 400 gm / 14 oz
Wholemilk fudge (*khoya*)	200 gm / 7 oz
Green cardamom (*choti elaichi*) powder	2 tsp / 6 gm
Screwpine (*kewra*) essence	2-3 drops
Saffron (*kesar*)	a few strands
Pistachios (*pista*) and almonds (*badaam*)	6 tsp
Silver leaves (*varq*)	a few

METHOD

Heat the milk in a heavy-bottomed pan; add the drained rice and bring to the boil on low heat. Do not stir.

Cook for about 1 hour or till the milk is reduced to half. Now start stirring, beat the milk with an electric beater for 2-3 minutes.

Keep stirring till the mixture becomes thick. Add sugar, wholemilk fudge, and green cardamom powder; cook for 2-3 minutes. Remove and keep aside to cool.

Add screwpine essence and mix well. Pour into individual bowls or in a serving dish and garnish with nuts, saffron, and silver leaves. Refrigerate for 2 hours or until chilled.

1583 to remove remaining obstacles on his march towards northwest and to deter others from advancing eastwards beyond this point.

The sights and sound of Lahore are a curious blend of Amritsar and Purani Dilli. Punjabiyat dominates here and pre-Partition nostalgia has a powerful hold.

VERMICELLI COOKED WITH DRIED DATES

INGREDIENTS

Vermicelli (*bareek sevain*)	175 gm / 6 oz
Dried dates (*chooharey*)	8-10
Full-cream milk	8 cups / 2 lt / 4 pints
Green cardamom	
(*choti elaichi*), powdered	3-4
Sugar	1¼ cups / 250 gm / 9 oz
Screwpine (*kewra*) essence	a few drops
Almonds (*badaam*),	
silvered	1 cup / 150 gm / 5 oz
Silver leaves (*varq*)	2

METHOD

Heat the milk in a pan; add powdered green cardamom and dried dates, cook until 6 cups of milk is left. Add vermicelli and cook for 10-15 minutes; add sugar stir and cook for 5 more minutes (the mixture should be like *kheer* not very thick). Remove from heat, add screwpine essence and mix well.

Transfer into a serving dish and garnish with almonds and silver leaves. Refrigerate for 2 hours before serving.

POTATO CUSTARD

INGREDIENTS

Milk	6 cups / 1½ lt / 3 pints
Potatoes, peeled,	
cut into 4 pieces	250 gm / 9 oz
Sugar	1¼ cups / 250 gm / 9 oz
Almonds (*badaam*)	2 tbsp / 30 gm / 1 oz
Pistachios (*pista*)	2 tbsp / 30 gm / 1 oz

METHOD

Boil the milk in a pot. Add the potatoes and cook till the potatoes are done and milk is reduced to half.

Add sugar and stir well till the mixture looks like *kheer*. No lumps of potato should be seen.

Add almonds and mix well. Remove and transfer into a serving dish and serve garnished with pistachios.

MURGH CHOLEY

CHICKEN COOKED WITH CHICKPEAS—LAHORI STYLE

INGREDIENTS

Chicken, cut into 8 pieces	I kg / 2.2 lb
Chickpeas (*kabuli chana*), soaked in 4 cups of cold water for 4 hours	2 cups / 300 gm / I I oz
Sodium bicarbonate	2 tbsp
Vegetable oil	2 tbsp / 30 ml / I fl oz
Onions, medium-sized, chopped	3
Ginger (*adrak*) paste	2 tsp / 12 gm
Garlic (*lasan*) paste	2 tsp / 12 gm
Red chilli powder	I tsp / 3 gm
Turmeric (*haldi*) powder	I tsp / 3 gm
Coriander (*dhaniya*) powder	I tsp / 3 gm
Tomatoes, medium-sized, chopped	3
Salt	I tsp / 3 gm
Yoghurt (*dahi*)	2 tbsp / 30 gm / I oz
Black cumin (*shahi jeera*) seeds	I tsp / 2½ gm
Garam masala powder	2 tsp / 6 gm
Chaat masala	2 tsp / 6 gm
Green chillies, chopped	4
Green coriander (*hara dhaniya*), chopped	½ cup / 25 gm
Ginger, chopped	2 tbsp / 24 gm

METHOD

Drain the chickpeas and sprinkle and rub in the cooking soda; leave aside for 10 minutes. Wash thoroughly in running tap water. Boil 4 cups of water in a pan, add the chickpeas and cook for about 1 hour or till tender.

Heat the oil in a pot; add the onions and sauté till golden. Add ginger and garlic pastes; stir for a minute. Add red chilli, turmeric and coriander powders; stir well.

Add tomatoes and stir for 2 minutes. Add salt and chicken and stir till the chicken is covered with the masala. Brown the chicken for a few seconds on high heat Reduce heat and simmer for 20 minutes or till the chicken is tender, the water has evaporated, and the oil separates.

Add yoghurt, boiled chickpeas and ½ cup of water; mix well. Add black cumin seeds, garam masala, *chaat* masala, and green chillies; mix well. Cook on low heat for 5 minutes. Remove and serve hot garnished with green coriander and ginger.

Facing page: Guests at one of the few surviving *sarais.* The times are tough and a man even at rest can ill afford to part with his gun and belt of bullets.

APRICOTS WITH VANILLA CUSTARD

INGREDIENTS

Apricots (*khoobani*), seedless	250 gm / 9 oz
Water	½ cup / 125 ml / 4 fl oz
Sugar	½ cup / 100 gm / 3½ oz
Almonds (*badaam*)	2 tbsp / 30 gm / 1 oz
Vanilla custard	1 cup
Cream, whipped	1 tbsp / 15 gm

METHOD

Boil the apricots in water, cover and cook on low heat till tender and are mashed fully, to make a thick purée. Add sugar and almonds.

Now make plain vanilla flavoured custard. Take 2 cups of milk and pour about 4 tbsp milk into a bowl. Add 2 tbsp of custard powder and mix thoroughly to make a smooth paste. Add 4 tbsp sugar to the remaining milk and boil in a saucepan, while stirring constantly add the contents of the bowl to the saucepan and cook for 2-3 minutes. Pour the custard in a bowl

In a serving dish put one layer of apricot mixture, then a layer of custard and finally a thin layer of whipped cream. Serve chilled.

Note: If using apricots with seed, soak overnight. Then cook as stated only take the seeds out when cooked.

Fate may have decreed the
    desert to our lot,
Blistered feet should deter us not,
Futile the barriers and
    erected walls—
The caravan of life can never
    be stopped.
Silence can only set the lips
    ablaze
Give voice to sparks that ignite
    your thoughts—
Life must learn the Lesson of Love,
Flowers fresh and myriad
    hued must bloom.

~Mohsin Bhopali,
Pakistani poet

The border between India and Pakistan, arbitrarily drawn in 1946-1947 by the British in a great haste to get out of the subcontinent after the Second World War, has failed to separate the people on the two sides. There are jingoist displays like the colourful closing ceremony at the Wagah Checkpost but the affinity of shared tastes remains strong.

Facing page: Spit and polish and bugles and brass. The ritual of the change of guard is performed daily with much fanfare and spirit of one-upmanship at the Wagah border by the Indian and Pakistani soldiers.

TANGRI KEBAB

STUFFED CHICKEN DRUMSTICKS

INGREDIENTS

Chicken drumsticks,	
cleaned, washed, pat dried, slit	16
For the stuffing:	
Butter	2 tbsp / 30 gm / 1 oz
Cashew nuts (*kaju*), roasted	1½ tbsp / 20 gm
Chicken, minced	400 gm / 14 oz
Salt to taste	
Yellow chilli powder	1 tsp / 3 gm
Garam masala powder	1 tsp / 3 gm
Green chillies, chopped	2 tsp / 10 gm
Green coriander	
(*hara dhaniya*), chopped	5 tbsp / 20 gm
Saffron (*kesar*)	a pinch
For the first marinade:	
Ginger-garlic	
(*adrak-lasan*) paste	1 tbsp / 18 gm

Lemon (*nimbu*) juice	2 tsp / 10 ml
White pepper	
(*safed mirch*) powder	1 tsp / 3 gm
Salt to taste	
For the second marinade:	
Processed cheese, grated	200 gm / 7 oz
Egg white	1
Cream	2 cups / 500 ml / 16 fl oz
Ginger-garlic paste	1 tsp / 6 gm
Salt to taste	
White pepper powder	1 tbsp / 9 gm
Green cardamom-mace	
(*elaichi-javitri*) powder	½ tsp / 1½ gm
Green chillies, chopped	1 tsp / 5 gm
Green coriander (*hara dhaniya*),	
chopped	1 tsp / 5 gm

Melted butter for basting

METHOD:

For the stuffing:

Heat the butter in a pan; add the cashew nuts and chicken mince; sauté until the meat turns white. Add the remaining ingredients and cook until the moisture evaporates and the mixture becomes completely dry. Remove from heat and cool. Divide this mixture into 16 equal portions and stuff each drumstick with this mixture. Make three incisions on the back side of the drumstick.

For the first marinade:

Mix all the ingredients mentioned and apply over the drumstick. Keep aside for 1 hour.

For the second marinade:

In a deep tray mix the cheese with the egg white gradually. Pour the cream and mix further so that it becomes a smooth paste. Add the remaining ingredients and mix. Mix the marinated chicken with this mixture. Keep aside for 2-3 hours.

Take a skewer and skew the chicken legs horizontally, leaving a gap of at least an inch between each leg. Roast in a moderately hot tandoor or over a charcoal grill for 10-12 minutes. Remove and hang so that the excess moisture drains out completely. Baste with melted butter and roast again for 3-4 minutes. Serve hot with salad.

Amritsar, the city, literally translated as a 'pool of nectar', derives its name from the sacred tank that surrounds the beautifully serene Golden Temple—the holiest shrine for the Sikhs. This is the first major 'destination' across the Pakistani border that the GT road touches on the Indian side. The Golden Temple that consecrates the entire city, was built by the fourth guru Ram Das more than four hundred years ago and its foundation stone was laid by a Sufi saint Miya Mir. This temple is the spiritual centre of the Sikh religion.

The Golden Temple. The blue-clad Nihang Sikhs are the soldiers in the service of the *Panth*—the Khalsa faith.

CHOOZA MAKHNI

CHICKEN DRUMSTICKS IN THICK TOMATO GRAVY

INGREDIENTS

Chicken legs, boneless, cut into 1¼" pieces	8

For the first marinade:

Garlic (lasan), strained	3½ tsp / 20 gm
Ginger (adrak) paste, strained	1¾ tsp / 10 gm
Lemon (nimbu) juice	¼ cup / 60 ml / 2 fl oz

For the second marinade:

Yoghurt (dahi), whisked	½ cup / 120 gm / 4 oz
Cream	2 tbsp / 30 ml / 1 fl oz
Garlic, strained	3½ tsp / 20 gm
Ginger, strained	1¾ tsp / 10 gm
Red chilli powder	1 tsp / 3 gm
Cumin (jeera) powder	½ tsp / 1½ gm
Black cardamom (moti elaichi) powder	1 tsp / 3 gm
Green cardamom (choti elaichi) powder	½ tsp / 1½ gm
Cinnamon (dalchini) powder	½ tsp / 1½ gm
Rose petal (gulaab pankhuri) powder	½ tsp / 1½ gm
Salt to taste	

For the gravy:

Butter	6 tbsp / 90 gm / 3 oz
Ginger paste	2½ tsp / 15 gm
Garlic paste	2½ tsp / 15 gm
Tomatoes, chopped	1 kg / 2.2 lb
Ginger, chopped	10 gm / 1" piece
Green chillies, slit, deseeded	2
Cashew nut (kaju) paste	3½ tsp / 20 gm
Salt to taste	
Red chilli powder	½ tsp / 1½ gm
Cream	10 tbsp / 150 ml / 5 fl oz
Garam masala powder	1 tsp / 3 gm
Dry fenugreek leaf (kasoori methi) powder	1 tsp

METHOD

For the first marinade:

Mix all the ingredients and rub the chicken evenly with this marinade. Reserve for 2 hours.

For the second marinade:

Mix all the ingredients. Rub the chicken with this marinade and reserve for 4 hours in the refrigerator.

Preheat the oven to 180°C / 350°F. Skewer the chicken pieces and roast keeping a tray underneath to collect the drippings.

For the gravy:

Melt ½ the butter in a pan; add ginger and garlic, and stir on medium heat until the moisture evaporates. Add tomatoes and salt; stir, cover and simmer until the tomatoes are mashed. Remove. Force the mixture through a fine mesh soup strainer into a separate pan and keep aside.

Melt the remaining butter in a saucepan; add ginger and green chillies. Sauté on medium heat for a minute. Add the grilled chicken and stir for a minute. Add the tomato purée and salt, bring to the boil. Reduce heat to low, add cashew nut paste and stir. Add red chilli powder and simmer until it reaches a thick-sauce like consistency. Remove, stir-in the cream and bring to the boil. Sprinkle garam masala and dry fenugreek leaf powders; stir well.

CHICKEN CUBES FLAVOURED WITH FRESH FENUGREEK

INGREDIENTS

Chicken leg, boneless, cut into 4 pieces,		Green coriander		
washed, pat-dried	850 gm / 30 oz	(*hara dhaniya*), chopped	2½ tbsp / 10 gm
Fenugreek leaves		Green chilli, chopped	½ tsp / 3 gm
(*methi*), fresh	250 gm / 8 oz	Ginger, chopped	1 tsp / 5 gm
Mustard (*sarson*) oil	¼ cup / 60 ml / 2 fl oz	Kashmiri red chilli powder	2 tbsp / 18 gm
Black cumin		Garam masala powder	1 tbsp / 9 gm
(*shahi jeera*) seeds	1 tsp / 2½ gm	*Chaat* masala	1 tbsp / 9 gm
For the first marinade:		Cornflour	2 tbsp / 20 gm
Ginger-garlic		Vegetable oil	1 tbsp / 15 ml
(*adrak-lasan*) paste	1 tbsp / 18 gm		
Lemon (*nimbu*) juice	2 tbsp / 30 ml / 1 fl oz	Melted butter for basting	
Salt to taste			
For the second marinade:			
Yoghurt (*dahi*),			
hung, whisked	1¼ cups / 300 gm / 11 oz		
Garlic paste	1 tbsp / 18 gm		
Dry fenugreek leaves			
(*kasoori methi*)	2 tbsp / 3 gm		

METHOD

In boiling water blanch the fenugreek leaves. Remove, drain the water and make a fine purée in a processor.

Heat the mustard oil in a pan; add the black cumin seeds. When it crackles, add fenugreek purée. Cook for a while and remove. Keep aside to cool.

For the first marinade:

Mix the ginger-garlic paste, 1 tbsp lemon juice, and salt together. Rub the marinade well over the chicken. Keep aside for 1 hour.

For the second marinade:

In a bowl mix all the ingredients. Add the cooked fenugreek purée, remaining lemon juice, cornflour, and oil; mix well. Adjust seasoning. Remove the excess moisture from the first marinade by squeezing the meat with the palm. Put the chicken pieces into the second marinade and rub well. Keep aside for 2-3 hours.

Take a skewer and skew the chicken pieces one by one. Keep a tray underneath to collect the drippings. Roast in a moderately hot tandoor or over a charcoal grill for 6-7 minutes, until half done. Remove and hang the skewer to let excess moisture drain out completely (2-3 minutes). Baste with melted butter and roast for another 3-4 minutes. Serve hot with choice of salad and chutney.

MURGH METHI

FENUGREEK CHICKEN

INGREDIENTS

Chicken, cut into 8 pieces	1	Ginger (*adrak*) paste	1 tsp / 6 gm
Tender fenugreek (*methi*) shoots	2 cups	Garlic (*lasan*) paste	1 tsp / 6 gm
Vegetable oil	100 ml / 3½ fl oz	Turmeric (*haldi*) powder	½ tsp / 1½ gm
Onions, large, cut in the middle horizontally, finely sliced vertically	3	Tomatoes, chopped	250 gm / 9 oz
		Salt to taste	
Green chillies, chopped	6	Red chilli powder	1 tsp / 3 gm

METHOD

Heat the oil in a heavy, wide-based pan; fry the onions till golden brown.

Add green chillies, ginger-garlic paste, and turmeric powder; sauté for a while.

Add chicken and fenugreek leaves and cook till the water somewhat dries up.

Add tomatoes, salt, and red chilli powder; sauté till the oil comes on the surface. Add just enough water to cook the chicken.

Cook on medium-low heat till the chicken is tender, leaving just a little gravy to coat the chicken.

The compound encloses the Akal Takht (the Sikh parliament) and the Harimandir Sahib. Built between 1589 and 1601 it presents a brilliant synthesis of Hindu and Islamic architecture. Virtually destroyed by an Afghan invader, Ahmed Shah Abdali, it was rebuilt some years later by Maharaja Ranjit Singh, the dynamic ruler of Punjab, who covered the dome in gold and lavishly embellished its interiors. It is also known as the Hari Mandir (Temple of God), which stands in the middle of the sacred pool, Amrit Sarovar (pool of nectar), and houses the Holy Book of the Sikhs, the *Guru*

Maharaja Ranjit Singh

LAMB COOKED WITH SPINACH

INGREDIENTS

Shoulder of kid / lamb (*dasti*), cut into 1½" boned cubes	750 gm / 1lb 11 oz
Spinach (*palak*), chopped	650 gm / 1lb 9 oz
Fenugreek (*methi*), fresh, chopped	150 gm / 5 oz
Ghee	½ cup / 100 gm / 3½ oz
Green cardamom (*choti elaichi*)	5
Cloves (*laung*)	4
Black cardamom (*moti elaichi*)	3
Cinnamon (*dalchini*), 1" sticks	2
Bay leaves (*tej patta*)	2
Onions, chopped	300 gm / 11 oz
Garlic (*lasan*), chopped	12 flakes
Ginger (*adrak*), chopped	15 gm / 1½" piece
Green chillies, deseeded, chopped	4
Salt to taste	

Red chilli powder	1 tsp / 3 gm
Turmeric (*haldi*) powder	1 tsp / 3 gm
Tomatoes, chopped	150 gm / 5 oz
Cream	2 tbsp / 30 ml / 1 oz
Cumin (*jeera*) seeds, freshly roasted, powdered	1½ tsp / 3 gm
Dry fenugreek leaf (*kasoori methi*) powder	a generous pinch
Ginger, juliennes; reserved in 1 tbsp lemon juice	10 gm / 1" piece

METHOD

Heat the ghee in a wok (*kadhai*); add green cardamom, cloves, black cardamom, cinnamon, and bay leaves; stir on medium heat until the green cardamom changes colour. Add the onions and the garlic; sauté until onions are light golden. Add ginger and green chillies, stir for a few seconds.

Add meat and sear on high heat for 2-3 minutes. Reduce to medium heat, add salt, red chilli and turmeric powders; stir. Reduce to low heat, cover and simmer until the meat releases all its juices. Uncover and stir-fry until the moisture evaporates.

Add tomatoes and stir-fry until the fat leaves the sides and the meat is almost cooked. Now add spinach and fresh fenugreek; stir-fry until the meat is cooked, and the liquid has evaporated and the spinach and fenugreek nappe the meat.

Stir in the cream and simmer for a minute. Sprinkle cumin and dry fenugreek leaf powder, stir. Remove and adjust the seasoning. Transfer to a serving dish, garnish with ginger juliennes and serve accompanied with chapatti, *roomali* or tandoori roti.

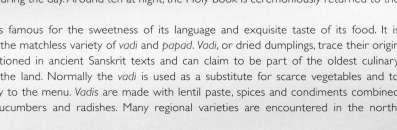

Granth Sahib, during the day. Around ten at night, the Holy Book is ceremoniously returned to the Akal Takht.

Amritsar is famous for the sweetness of its language and exquisite taste of its food. It is renowned for the matchless variety of *vadi* and *papad*. *Vadi*, or dried dumplings, trace their origin to *vatika* mentioned in ancient Sanskrit texts and can claim to be part of the oldest culinary repertoire of the land. Normally the *vadi* is used as a substitute for scarce vegetables and to provide variety to the menu. *Vadis* are made with lentil paste, spices and condiments combined with grated cucumbers and radishes. Many regional varieties are encountered in the north.

KEEMA CHOLEY

CHICKPEAS AND KID / LAMB MINCE TIMBALE

INGREDIENTS

Chickpeas (kabuli chana)	½ cup / 75 gm / 1½ oz
Soda bicarbonate	a pinch
Salt to taste	
Ghee	2 tbsp / 30 gm / 1 oz
Ginger (adrak), strained	1¾ tsp / 10 gm
Garlic (lasan), strained	1¾ tsp / 10 gm
Mango powder (amchur)	½ tsp / 1½ gm
Black pepper (kaali mirch), roasted, coarsely ground	½ tsp / 1½ gm
Cumin (jeera) powder	¼ tsp
Cinnamon (dalchini) powder	¼ tsp
Black cardamom (moti elaichi) powder	¼ tsp
Nutmeg (jaiphal) powder	¼ tsp

Black rock salt (kaala namak)	a pinch
Dry fenugreek leaf (kasoori methi) powder	a pinch

For the bouquet garni (potli):

Black cardamom	4
Green cardamom (choti elaichi)	4
Cinnamon (dalchini) sticks	2
Bay leaves (tej patta)	2

For the mince:

Kid / Lamb mince (keema)	600 gm / 22 oz
Ghee	6 tbsp / 90 gm / 3 oz
Onions, finely chopped	¾ cup / 90 gm / 3 oz
Garlic, strained	5 tsp / 30 gm / 1 oz
Ginger, strained	3¼ tsp / 20 gm

Tomato purée, fresh	200 gm / 7 oz
Kashmiri red chilli (deghi mirch) powder	1 tsp / 3 gm
Black pepper, freshly roasted, coarsely ground	½ tsp / 1½ gm
Clove (laung) powder	a pinch
Black cardamom (moti elaichi) powder	a pinch
Green cardamom powder	a pinch
Cinnamon (dalchini) powder	a pinch
Mace (javitri) powder	a pinch
Processed cheese, grated	30 gm / 1 oz

For the filling:

Almonds (badaam), blanched, peeled, cut into slivers	16
Pistachios (pista), blanched, peeled, cut into slivers	
Raisins (kishmish)	16
Green chillies, finely chopped	2
Mint (pudina) leaves, washed	30 gm / 1 oz
Processed cheddar cheese, grated	

In Bengal too *bodi* is used. In Kashmir it is primarily used for spicing. But it is in Punjab that the *vadi* comes into its own. The city of Amritsar has no peers as far as the amazing array of *vadis* available are concerned. There are gems like the *alubukhara vadi* or plum dumplings that contain within them a dried plum and others that are bejewelled with pomegranate seeds.

The Holy City has drawn a stream of visitors for centuries who have brought with them a diversity of culinary influences. The food, both vegetarian and non-vegetarian, is truly resplendent. The *Guru ka langar*, the community kitchen, run at the Golden Temple has passed on the tradition of pure and nourishing repast even to street-side food stalls. The fare is most basic—lentils and

METHOD

For the bouquet garni:

Put all the ingredients in a mortar and pound with a pestle to break the spices, fold in a piece of muslin and secure with a long enough string for it to hang over the rim of the pan.

Cook the chickpeas in 4 cups of water, bring to the boil. Continue to boil for 2 minutes; remove and reserve in the same water overnight. Drain just prior to cooking. Put the drained chickpeas in a pot, add soda bicarbonate, salt and 4 cups of water, bring to the boil. Reduce heat to low, add the bouquet garni, cover and simmer until al dente (cooked but not mushy). Drain, remove and discard the bouquet garni.

Melt the ghee in a wok (*kadhai*); add ginger and garlic, stir on medium heat until the moisture evaporates. Add the drained chickpeas, stir gently for 4-5 minutes (ensuring that they do not break). Sprinkle all the spices, stir carefully to incorporate and divide into 4 equal portions.

For the mince:

Melt the ghee in a wok; sauté the onions on medium heat until light golden. Add garlic and ginger, and sauté until onions are golden. Add the mince, stir-fry for 2-3 minutes. Add tomato purée, stir. Add red chilli powder and salt, stir-fry until the fat leaves the sides. Sprinkle all the spices and mix well. Remove and keep aside to cool. When cool, add cheese, mix well and divide into 4 equal portions.

For the filling:

Mix all the ingredients in a bowl and divide into 4 equal portions.

Arrange 4 pie rings of 4$\frac{1}{2}$" diameter on a baking tray, spread a portion of the mince in each, spread a portion of the filling and, finally, top with a portion of the chickpeas. Cook in a preheated oven (140°C / 275°F) for 8-10 minutes.

TENDER LAMB CUBES

INGREDIENTS

Shoulder of kid / lamb	
(*dasti*), boned, ¼" cubes	1.2 kg / 2¼ lb
For the marinade:	
Ghee	2 tbsp / 30 gm / 1 oz
Green cardamom (*choti elaichi*)	6
Cloves (*laung*)	6
Black cardamom (*moti elaichi*)	3
Cinnamon (*dalchini*), 1" sticks	3
Garlic (*lasan*), strained	5 tsp / 30 gm / 1 oz
Ginger (*adrak*), strained	3½ tsp / 20 gm
Yoghurt (*dahi*),	
whisked	1¼ cups / 250 gm / 9 oz
Red chilli powder	2 tsp / 6 gm
Onions, fried till crisp and	
brown	100 gm / 3½ oz
Salt to taste	
Ghee	½ cup / 100 gm / 3½ oz

Garlic flakes, chopped	8
Onions, chopped	1½ cups / 180 gm / 6 oz
Ginger, chopped	15 gm / 1½" piece
Green chillies, deseeded, chopped	4
Tomatoes, large, chopped	3
Cumin (*jeera*) powder	1½ tsp / 4½ gm
Black pepper (*kaali mirch*),	
roasted, coarsely ground	1½ tsp / 4½ gm
Black cardamom powder	½ tsp / 1½ gm
Clove powder	¼ tsp
Cinnamon, 1" stick	¼ tsp
Salt to taste	
Dark Rum (XXX)	2 tbsp / 30 ml / 1 fl oz
Green coriander	
(*hara dhaniya*), chopped	3 tbsp / 12 gm
Lemon (*nimbu*) juice	1 tbsp / 15 ml
Dry fenugreek leaf	
(*kasoori methi*) powder	1 tsp / 3 gm

METHOD:

For the marinade:

Mix all the ingredients in a pan, evenly rub the meat with this marinade and reserve for at least 2 hours. Transfer the pan to the heat and stir-fry on medium heat. When the juices begin to boil, reduce heat to low and stir-fry until the meat is cooked and the juices have evaporated. Remove and keep aside. (Add small quantities of water if necessary to prevent sticking.)

Spread the ghee on a griddle (*tawa*); add garlic and sauté on medium heat until light golden. Add onions and sauté until the onions become translucent and glossy. Add ginger and green chillies, stir for a few seconds. Add tomatoes and stir-fry until they become soft (release their juices).

Add the cooked meat and stir-fry until the masala nappes the meat. Sprinkle the spice powders; stir. Add salt, stir. Now add rum, turn with a spatula to incorporate, add green coriander, lemon juice, and dry fenugreek leaf powder; stir. Remove and adjust the seasoning.

Transfer to a flat dish and serve as a cocktail snack, or as a starter, or as an entrée with chapatti or tandoori roti.

Facing page: The food in Amritsar is enriched routinely with nuts and dry fruits. The city has many shops specializing in these.

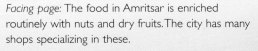

AMRITSARI MACHCHI

DEEP-FRIED FISH FILLETS

INGREDIENTS

Fish fillets (*Singhara / Malli / Sole*),	
washed, pat-dried	2 (I kg / 2¼ lb each)
Mustard (*sarson*) oil for deep-frying	

For the batter:

Gram flour (*besan*)	45 gm / 1½ oz
Garlic (*lasan*), strained	5¼ tsp / 30 gm / I oz
Ginger (*adrak*) paste, strained	3½ tsp / 20 gm
Red chilli powder	I tsp / 3 gm
Carom seeds (*ajwain*)	I tsp / 2½ gm
Asafoetida (*hing*)	a generous pinch

Salt to taste	

For the masala:

Cumin (*jeera*) seeds	65 gm / 2¼ oz
Black peppercorns (*sabut kaali*	
mirch)	65 gm / 2¼ oz
Black rock salt (*kaala namak*)	60 gm / 2 oz
Dry mint (*pudina*) leaves	30 gm / I oz
Carom seeds	2 tsp / 5 gm
Asafoetida	I tsp / 5 gm
Tartric	¾ tsp / 4 gm
Mango powder (*amchur*)	100 gm / 3½ oz
Salt to taste	
Ginger powder (*sonth*)	2 tbsp / 20 gm
Yellow chilli powder	2 tbsp / 20 gm

METHOD

For the batter:

Put all the ingredients in a large bowl. Add ¼ cup of water and mix to make a thin batter. Evenly rub the fillets with this batter and reserve in the bowl for 30 minutes.

For the masala:

Put all the ingredients (except mango powder, salt, ginger powder and yellow chilli powder) in a mortar and pound with a pestle to make a fine powder. Transfer to clean, dry bowl, add the remaining ingredients and mix well. Sieve and store in a sterilized, dry and airtight container.

Heat the mustard oil in a wok (*kadhai*); deep-fry the fish in convenient batches on medium heat until light golden. Remove and drain the excess oil on absorbent paper towels and cool. When cool, make one slit down the middle along the length and 4 slits across the breadth. Then reheat the oil and deep-fry the fish again until golden and crusty. Remove and drain the excess oil.

Place a paper doiley on a platter, arrange the fillets on top, sprinkle the prepared masala and serve with grated radish-in-mint-chutney and lemon wedges.

chapatti, and all the cooking and serving is done by volunteers. The large dining hall can seat 3,000 diners at one time and the kitchen is equipped to serve 10,000 people a day. The *langar* is a common feature at all Sikh gurudwaras. Guru Nanak, the founder of the Sikh religion, preached equality and conceived the idea of a *langar* to promote a casteless egalitarian society. Caste taboos, the Guru knew, become inhuman and social discrimination is most painful on occasions like public dining. The use of volunteers in the kitchen also emphasizes the idea of *kar seva*, so dear to the Guru. The dignity of labour and putting service before self, dedication to a cause are all learnt best not by preaching but practice. The prasad at the Golden Temple is called *kada prasad* (a halwa

SPICY LAMB BRAIN

INGREDIENTS

Kid / Lamb brains, cleaned,	
remove the sinews, washed, pat-dried	8
Milk	2 cups / 500 ml / 16 fl oz
Brandy	3 tbsp / 45 ml / 1½ fl oz
Turmeric (haldi) powder	1 tsp / 3 gm
Black cardamom (moti elaichi)	4
Cloves (laung)	4
Cinnamon (dalchini), 1" sticks	2
Bay leaves (tej patta)	3
Ghee	5 tbsp / 75 gm / 2½ oz
Garlic (lasan), strained	1¾ tsp / 10 gm
Onions, washed,	
finely chopped	2 cups / 250 gm / 9 oz
Ginger (adrak) paste, strained	3½ tsp / 20 gm
Green chillies, deseeded,	
cut into juliennes	2
Yoghurt (dahi),	
whisked	2 cups / 500 gm / 1.1 lb

Coriander (dhaniya) powder	1 tsp / 3 gm
Red chilli powder	2 tsp / 6 gm
Turmeric (haldi) powder	½ tsp / 1½ gm
Cashew nut (kaju) paste	2 tbsp / 30 gm / 1 oz
Green cardamom	
(choti elaichi) powder	½ tsp / 1½ gm
Black cumin (shahi jeera)	
powder	½ tsp / 1½ gm
Cinnamon powder	⅛ tsp
Clove powder	⅛ tsp
Fennel (saunf) powder	2 tsp / 3 gm
Salt to taste	
Green coriander	
(hara dhaniya), chopped	1 tbsp / 4 gm
Lemon (nimbu) juice	2 tsp / 10 ml

METHOD

Put the brains in a panful of milk, add brandy and reserve overnight in the refrigerator.

Bring a panful of water to the boil with turmeric powder, black cardamom, cloves, cinnamon sticks, and bay leaves. Drain and add brain, and boil for 2 minutes. Remove and keep aside.

Spread the ghee in a pan. Add garlic, sauté on medium heat with a spatula until light golden. Add onions and sauté until onions become translucent and glossy. Add ginger and green chillies, stir for a few seconds. Add the yoghurt mixture, stir-fry until the fat leaves the sides. Add the cashew nut paste and stir-fry until the fat leaves the side. Then add 2 cups of water and bring to the boil. Reduce heat to low, sprinkle green cardamom, black cumin, cinnamon, clove and fennel powders; stir. Add salt, stir, cover with a lid and cook on dum for 20 minutes. Then add the cooked brain and stir-fry, simultaneously 'chopping' the brain with the spatula into ¾" pieces, until the masala nappes the brain. Add green coriander and stir, turning with the spatula to incorporate. Remove, sprinkle lemon juice, stir, and adjust the seasoning.

made with equal amounts of flour, ghee, and sugar). The name is traced to the large kadhai (wok) or the cooking vessels in which it is prepared.

The dhabas along the GT road are arguably the best eating places in the land. They are roadside eateries on the highway that were originally set up by the refugees from west Punjab after Partition. The dhaba started not as a restaurant or a business proposition, but as a strategy for survival in 1947-1948. These down-to-earth eateries have assumed a pan-Indian identity. The

Guru Ram Das overseeing the enlargement of a pond at Guru ka Chak depicted in a panel in Harimandir Sahib.

BATAER MASALEDAAR

SPICY QUAILS

INGREDIENTS

Quails (*bataer*), prick the surface with a fork   8

For the marinade:

Red wine	6 tbsp / 90 ml / 3 fl oz
Malt vinegar (*sirka*)	2 tbsp / 30 ml / 1 fl oz
Garlic (*lasan*), strained	45 gm / 1½ oz
Ginger (*adrak*), strained	5¼ tsp / 30 gm
Red chilli powder	1½ tsp / 4½ gm
Salt to taste	

For the filling:

Chicken, minced	250 gm / 9 oz
Garlic, finely chopped	8 flakes
Ginger, finely chopped	7½ gm / ¾" piece
Green chillies, finely chopped	2
Pistachios (*pista*), roasted	16
Raisins (*kishmish*), refreshed in water until they puff up	16
Black cumin seeds (*shahi jeera*)	½ tsp / 1¼ gm
Black pepper (*kaali mirch*), freshly roasted, coarsely ground	¾ tsp
Green cardamom (*choti elaichi*) powder	½ tsp / 1½ gm
Mace (*javitri*) powder	¼ tsp
Salt to taste	

For the gravy:

Ghee	6 tbsp / 75 gm / 2½ oz
Black cardamom (*moti elaichi*)	4
Cloves (*laung*)	4
Cinnamon (*dalchini*), 1" sticks	2
Bay leaves (*tej patta*)	2
Garlic flakes, finely chopped	8
Onions, grated	250 gm / 9 oz
Ginger, finely chopped	10 gm / 1" piece
Coriander (*dhaniya*) powder	2 tsp / 6 gm
Red chilli powder	1 tsp / 3 gm
Tomatoes, finely chopped	200 gm / 7 oz
Salt to taste	
Yoghurt (*dahi*), whisked	75 gm / 2½ oz
Almond (*badaam*) paste	30 gm / 1 oz

Green cardamom powder	½ tsp / 1½ gm
Cinnamon powder	¼ tsp
Clove powder	¼ tsp
Mace powder	¼ tsp
Saffron (*kesar*)	½ tsp

For the garnishing:

Saffron, crushed with a pestle, soaked in lukewarm water	¼ tsp
Almonds flakes, toasted and added to saffron water	
Silver leaves (*varq*)	a few

cooking style is predominantly tandoori, the menu is limited, ingredients used are fresh and the food served is no-frills, home-like and great value for money. The tandoori classics are—tandoori chicken, butter chicken, fried *dal makhani*, *choley*, *paneer*, *karhi*, *baingan ka bharta*, *saag* (with and without meat) and *bhurji* made with eggs or cottage cheese. Accompaniments to this are: thick rich yoghurt and a most elementary salad of onion, green chillies, and lemon.

Kar sevaks (volunteers) at the *langar*—community kitchen.

METHOD:

For the marinade:

Mix all the ingredients together, evenly rub the marinade over the quails and reserve for at least an hour.

For the filling:

Mix all the ingredients and divide into 8 equal portions. Stuff the abdominal cavity of the quails with a portion of the filling from the tail end, then double up the legs, ensuring that the drumsticks cover the opening through which the filling was stuffed and tie firmly with a string. Gently twist the winglet bones to make the birds more stable when they are placed on the plate at the time of service.

For the gravy:

Heat the ghee in a pan; add black cardamom, cloves, cinnamon sticks, and bay leaves. Stir on medium heat for a few seconds. Add garlic and sauté until it begins to change colour. Add onions and sauté until onions are light golden. Add ginger, stir-fry until onions are golden, add coriander powder and red chilli powder dissolved in 2 tbsp of water, and stir-fry until the moisture evaporates.

Then add tomatoes and salt, and stir-fry until the fat leaves the sides. Remove the pan from the heat, stir-in yoghurt, return the pan to heat, stir-fry on medium heat until specs of fat begin to appear on the surface. Add almond paste, stir-fry until the fat leaves the sides, add approximately 4 cups of water, bring to the boil. Reduce heat to medium, add the quails, bring to the boil again. Reduce heat to low heat, cover and simmer, stirring occasionally, but carefully, until the quails are almost cooked. Uncover, increase heat to medium and cook until the gravy is of medium-thick sauce like consistency. Sprinkle green cardamom, cinnamon, clove and mace powders; stir. Add saffron, stir, remove and adjust the seasoning.

Place 2 quails on each of the 4 individual plate. Serve garnished with almond flakes in saffron water, silver leaves and accompanied with bread of your choice.

Kesar Da Dhaba and Bhrawan Da Dhaba are the two *dhabas* that have moved upscale imitating family restaurants but there are countless others that match their food. Whatever you eat is served with a generous dollop of *ghee*. As if this were not enough all this is washed down with a large tumbler full of *lassi* (creamy yoghurt drink) sweetened with *peda* (sweetmeat) if you like. Lawrence Street is the food mall where countless small vans and movable stalls specialize in different delicacies. Some have built a reputation on a single dish. Those that belong undisputably to the 'must taste' category are the *tawa* tikka and *bharwaan kulche*. *Amritsari machchi* is as much a part of the city's legacy as the biryani in Hyderabad.

DAL MAKHANI

BLACK GRAM ENRICHED WITH BUTTER, CREAM AND TOMATO PURÉE

INGREDIENTS

Black gram (*urad dal*), whole, washed in running water, soaked overnight, drained	1 cup / 200 gm / 7 oz
Vegetable oil	2 tbsp / 30 gm / 1 fl oz
Garlic (*lasan*), strained	5 tsp / 30 ml / 1 fl oz
Ginger (*adrak*) paste, strained	3¼ tsp / 20 gm
Red chilli powder	1 tbsp / 9 gm
Salt to taste	
Tomato purée	2 cups / 400 gm / 14 oz
Butter, unsalted	180 gm / 6 oz
Cream	½ cup / 120 ml / 4 fl oz

METHOD

Cook the drained black gram in a pan, with 12 cups of water. Add oil and bring to the boil.

Reduce heat to low, cover and simmer until cooked (for approximately 4 hours). Add garlic, ginger, red chilli powder, and salt, stirring continuously and mashing the black gram against the sides with a wooden spoon and, as you do that incorporate scraps of the black gram that cling to the sides as the liquid diminishes (approximately 1 hour).

Add tomato purée and 150 gm / 5 oz of butter, continue to cook. Stir-in the cream, remove and adjust the seasoning. Serve garnished with the remaining butter.

After feasting in style on the streets of Amritsar a siesta is in order as the journey to the next food stop for the driver and refuelling for the vehicle lies about just another hundred odd miles away. The city of Ludhiana is the cycle and the motorcycle capital of the world. The Hero Group is the largest manufacturer of bicycles and motorcycles and figures prominently in The *Guiness Book of Records*. The city is named after an old fort built by the Lodhis—the dynasty that ruled India before the advent of the Mughals—that lies in the vicinity of the modern city. Ludhiana is indeed an industrial power house—home to hosiery and woollens that form a large part of Indian exports, machine and machine tools, and food products. Like the neighbouring city of Jallandhar, Ludhiana too has prospered primarily

RED KIDNEY BEANS IN A TOMATO GRAVY

India / Punjab / Amritsar

INGREDIENTS

Red kidney beans (*rajma*), washed, soaked overnight	1¼ cups / 250 gm / 9 oz
Black cardamom (*moti elaichi*)	4
Bay leaves (*tej patta*)	2
Ghee	6 tbsp / 90 gm / 3 oz
Dry red chillies (*sookhi lal mirch*)	4
Cumin (*jeera*) seeds	1½ tsp / 3 gm
Onions, finely chopped	1⅔ cups / 180 gm / 6 oz
Garlic (*lasan*) paste, strained	5 tsp / 30 gm / 1 oz
Ginger (*adrak*) paste, strained	5 tsp / 30 gm / 1 oz
Coriander (*dhaniya*) powder	1 tsp / 3 gm
Red chilli powder	1 tsp / 3 gm
Salt to taste	
Tomato purée, fresh	1 cup / 200 gm / 7 oz
Black cardamom (*moti elaichi*) powder	1 tsp / 3 gm
Black pepper (*kaali mirch*) powder	½ tsp / 1½ gm
Salt to taste	

For the garnishing:

Ginger, cut into juliennes	10 gm / 1" piece
Green coriander (*hara dhaniya*), finely chopped	2 tbsp / 8 gm

METHOD

Boil the red kidney beans in 6½ cups of water. Remove the scum, reduce heat to low and add black cardamom and bay leaves, boil until cooked. Remove black cardamom and bay leaves.

Heat the ghee in a pan; add dry red chillies and cumin seeds, stir on medium heat until the seeds begin to crackle. Add onions and sauté until light golden. Add garlic and ginger pastes, sauté until golden brown.

Add coriander powder, red chilli powder, and salt (all dissolved in ¼ cup of water), stir for 30 seconds. Add tomato purée and stir-fry until the fat leaves the sides. Add the boiled kidney beans and bring to the boil. Reduce heat to low and cook for 6-7 minutes. Sprinkle black cardamom and black pepper powders and stir. Remove and adjust the seasoning.

Transfer the dish into a serving bowl, serve garnished with ginger and green coriander and accompanied with steamed rice.

due to the GT Road. Many of the richest denizens of Ludhiana are refugees who had drifted into the city after Partition. The glitzy shopping malls that greet the visitor today bear testimony to their grit and determination, their vision and entrepreneurship. They work hard and play equally hard, their love of food is legendary.

Chicken is almost a staple. You may order a butter chicken, a *tangri kebab*, *murgh malai tikka* or a *reshmi kebab*—you will never be disappointed. And if you prefer the reddish meat, you can sample

Vignettes from the lives of the Gurus portrayed in the panel at the Harimandir Sahib.

PINDI CHANA

CHICKPEAS COOKED DRY

INGREDIENTS

Chickpeas (*kabuli chana*), soaked for 1 hour	400 gm /14 oz
Soda bicarbonate	a generous pinch
Vegetable oil	5 tbsp / 75 ml / 2½ fl oz
Carom seeds (*ajwain*)	1 tsp / 2½ gm
Gram flour (*besan*)	1 tbsp / 10 gm
Pomegranate (*anaar dana*) powder	5 tsp / 15 gm
Mango powder (*amchur*)	2 tsp / 6 gm
Red chilli powder	1 tsp / 3 gm
Black rock salt (*kaala namak*) powder	1 tsp / 3 gm
Dry fenugreek leaf (*kasoori methi*) powder	2 tsp
Cumin (*jeera*) powder	1 tsp / 3 gm
Salt to taste	

For the bouquet garni (*potli*):

Black cardamom (*moti elaichi*)	6
Cinnamon (*dalchini*) powder	4 sticks
Cloves (*laung*)	4
Ginger (*adrak*), crushed	20 gm / 2" piece
Tea leaves	2 tsp / 5 gm

For the garnish:

Tomatoes, medium-sized, cut into wedges	
Onion, medium-sized, cut into roundels & rings separated	1
Green chillies, slit, deseeded	2
Lemons (*nimbu*), cut into wedges	3
Ginger, juliennes, soaked in 2 tbsp lemon juice	10 gm / 1" piece

METHOD

Bring the chickpeas to the boil. Continue to boil for 2 minutes, remove and reserve in the same water for an hour. Drain just prior to cooking.

For the bouquet garni:
Put all the ingredients in a small piece of muslin and secure with a string to make a pouch.

Add 4 cups of fresh water to the drained chickpeas, bring to the boil. Reduce heat to low, and remove the scum. Add 1½ tbsp oil and the bouquet garni, cover and simmer until cooked but firm (make sure that neither the chickpeas gets mashed, nor the skin starts to peel). Remove and keep aside.

Heat the remaining oil in a wok (*kadhai*); add carom seeds and stir on medium heat until it begins to crackle. Add gram flour and stir-fry until it emits its unique aroma. Then add the remaining ingredients, stir for a minute. Add the boiled chickpeas and stir until well mixed. Remove and adjust the seasoning.

Remove to a serving dish, garnish with tomatoes, onion rings, green chillies, lemon, and ginger. Serve with *bhatura* or *kulcha*.

some excellent *achari gosht*, *saag gosht*, *keema kaleji* or *magaz masala*. *Butter chicken* is the classic case of the ugly duckling transforming magically into a swan. What started as a recipe to reuse a leftover *tandoori* chicken has over the years evolved into an international favourite. It is seldom based on a precooked tandoori chicken now and is delicately assembled from scratch. The discerning diner is no longer content with a mildly sweet and sour rich tomato gravy, but looks for aromatics like fenugreek, cardamom, and cinnamon. The reasons for the popularity of butter chicken are not hard to see. It is colourful, gentle on the palate and the health conscious can cut the fat and be content with the butter only in name.

CRUMBLED COTTAGE CHEESE WITH GREEN CHICKPEAS

INGREDIENTS

Green chickpeas (*cholia*), boiled until al dente	300 gm / 10 oz
Cottage cheese (*paneer*), crumbled	450 gm / 1 lb
Ghee	¼ cup / 50 gm / 1¾ oz
Cumin (*jeera*) seeds	1 tsp / 2 gm
Onions, chopped	¾ cup / 90 gm / 3 oz
Ginger (*adrak*) paste	2½ tsp / 15 gm
Garlic (*lasan*) paste	2½ tsp / 15 gm
Kashmiri red chilli (*deghi mirch*) powder	1 tsp / 3 gm
Turmeric (*haldi*) powder	½ tsp / 1½ gm
Tomatoes, chopped	1 cup / 175 gm / 6 oz
Green chillies, seeded, cut into ⅛"-thick strips	4
Salt to taste	
Black pepper (*kaali mirch*) powder, coarsely ground	1 tsp / 3 gm
Green cardamom (*choti elaichi*) powder	a generous pinch
Clove (*laung*) powder	a generous pinch
Nutmeg (*jaiphal*) powder	a generous pinch
Dry fenugreek leaf (*kasoori methi*) powder	a generous pinch
Ginger, cut into juliennes	15 gm / 1½" piece
Green coriander (*hara dhaniya*), finely chopped	¼ cup / 12½ gm

METHOD

Heat the ghee in a wok (*kadhai*); add cumin seeds and stir on medium heat until it begins to pop. Add onions, sauté until light golden. Add the ginger and garlic pastes, stir-fry until the moisture evaporates. Add red chilli and turmeric powders (dissolved in 2 tbsp water), and stir-fry until the moisture evaporates. Add tomatoes, stir-fry until the moisture evaporates.

Add green chickpeas and cook until the fat leaves the sides. Add cottage cheese, green chillies, and salt; stir-fry for a minute. Add black pepper, green cardamom, clove, nutmeg and fenugreek leaf powders; stir. Remove and adjust the seasoning.

Transfer to a flat dish, garnished with ginger and green coriander. Serve with chapatti.

BAINGAN KA BHARTA

MASHED AUBERGINES

INGREDIENTS

Aubergines (*baingan*)	4
Vegetable oil to brush the aubergines	
Garlic (*lasan*)	8
Cloves (*laung*)	8
Ghee	½ cup / 100 gm / 3½ oz
Cumin (*jeera*) seeds	1 tsp / 2 gm
Onions, chopped	2 cups / 250 gm / 9 oz
Ginger (*adrak*), chopped	10 gm / 1" piece
Green chillies, deseeded, chopped	4
Red chilli powder	1 tsp / 3 gm
Turmeric (*haldi*) powder	½ tsp / 1½ gm
Tomatoes, chopped	350 gm / 12 oz
Salt to taste	
Green coriander (*hara dhaniya*), chopped	2 tbsp / 8 gm

METHOD

Stud each aubergine with 2 flakes of garlic and 2 cloves, and brush with ghee. Roast the aubergines on embers of charcoal, on an *angeethi* or tandoor, and turn at regular intervals, until the skin becomes black. You can also roast on low heat on a gas range. Remove, discard the cloves, transfer to a panful of water, cool, peel the blackened skin and mash the flesh.

Heat the ghee in a wok *(kadhai)*; add cumin seeds and stir on medium heat until it begins to pop. Add onions, and sauté until transparent. Then add ginger and green chillies, sauté for a few seconds. Add aubergine, red chilli and turmeric powders; stir-fry until fat leaves the sides. Now add tomatoes and salt, continue to cook until fat leaves the sides. Remove and adjust the seasoning.

Transfer to a serving dish, garnish with green coriander and serve with tandoori paratha.

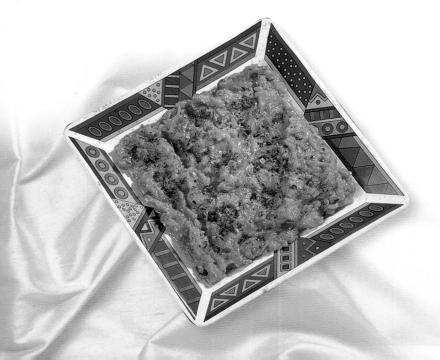

Let us not give you the impression that it is only the carnivores who have all the fun. The vegetarians have seasonal delights that are equally satisfying. Winter is welcomed with *makki ki roti* (maize flour bread) and *sarson ka saag* (mustard greens), a combo meal that is supposed to be extremely nutritious. The word *saag* means leafy green vegetables and, in this case, is usually a blend of mustard, spinach, and *bathua*. The greens are cooked on a slow fire and mashed to a porridge-like consistency. It is not uncommon to add to the body a few radishes or turnips. The roti is not rolled with a rolling pin but shaped lovingly by hand. Lovers of tradition also insist on using only

KADHAI PANEER

SERVES: 4-6

STIR-FRIED COTTAGE CHEESE WITH BELL PEPPER

INGREDIENTS

For the cottage cheese:

Cottage cheese (*paneer*), cut into 2" x ½" x ½" batons	800 gm / 1 lb 13 oz
Ghee	3 tbsp / 45 gm / 1½ oz
Onions, chopped	¾ cup / 90 gm / 3 oz
Garlic (*lasan*) paste	3½ tsp / 20 gm
Ginger (*adrak*) paste	1¾ tsp / 10 gm
Coriander (*dhaniya*) seeds, roasted, pounded to split	1 tsp / 2 gm
Black pepper (*kaali mirch*), freshly roasted, coarsely ground	1 tsp / 3 gm
Red chilli powder	1 tsp / 3 gm
Turmeric (*haldi*) powder	½ tsp / 1½ gm
Tomato purée	1½ cups / 360 gm / 13 oz
Salt to taste	
Green pepper (*Shimla mirch*), cut into ⅛"-thick strips	1
Yellow bell pepper, cut into ⅛"-thick strips	1
Red bell peppers, cut into ⅛"-thick strips	1
Cumin (*jeera*) powder	¾ tsp / 2¼ gm
Green cardamom (*choti elaichi*) powder	½ tsp / 1½ gm
Mace (*javitri*) powder	⅛ tsp
Cinnamon (*dalchini*) powder	⅛ tsp
Clove (*laung*) powder	⅛ tsp
Dry fenugreek leaf (*kasoori methi*) / Fenugreek seeds (*methi dana*)	a pinch
Green coriander (*hara dhaniya*), chopped	1 tbsp / 4 gm

METHOD

Heat the ghee in a pan; add onions and sauté until translucent and glossy. Add garlic and ginger pastes, and stir-fry until the moisture evaporates. Add coriander seeds and black pepper, stir-fry until the coriander begins to change colour. Add red chilli and turmeric powders dissolved in 2 tbsp of water, and stir-fry until the moisture evaporates.

Add tomato purée and salt, stir-fry until specks of fat begin to appear on the surface. Add cottage cheese, stir for a minute. Add the bell peppers and stir for a minute. Sprinkle the cumin, green cardamom, mace, cinnamon, clove, and dry fenugreek leaf powders; stir carefully. Remove and adjust the seasoning.

Transfer to a serving dish, garnish with green coriander and serve with tandoori roti or chapatti.

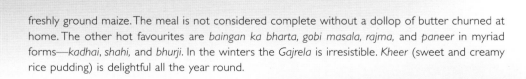

freshly ground maize. The meal is not considered complete without a dollop of butter churned at home. The other hot favourites are *baingan ka bharta, gobi masala, rajma,* and *paneer* in myriad forms—*kadhai, shahi,* and *bhurji*. In the winters the *Gajrela* is irresistible. *Kheer* (sweet and creamy rice pudding) is delightful all the year round.

ALOO VADIYAN

POTATOES COOKED WITH DRIED BLACK GRAM DUMPLINGS

INGREDIENTS

Potatoes, cut into thin long strips	4	Coriander (*dhaniya*) powder	1 tbsp / 9 gm
Vadi (made of black gram; deep-fried		Red chilli powder	1 tsp / 3 gm
in oil and reserved in water)	250 gm / 9 oz	Turmeric (*haldi*) powder	1 tsp / 3 gm
Ghee	5 tbsp / 75 gm / 2½ oz	Tomato purée, fresh	150 gm / 5 oz
Cumin (*jeera*) seeds	2 tsp / 4 gm	Salt to taste	
Onions, chopped	150 gm / 5 oz	Dry fenugreek leaf (*kasoori methi*)	
Ginger (*adrak*) paste	3½ tsp / 20 gm	powder	a generous pinch
Garlic (*lasan*) paste	1¾ tsp / 10 gm	Green coriander (*hara dhaniya*),	
Yoghurt (*dahi*)	150 gm / 5 oz	chopped	1 tbsp / 4 gm

METHOD

Heat the ghee in a wok (*kadhai*); add cumin seeds and stir on medium heat until it begins to pop. Add onions, sauté until light golden. Add garlic and ginger pastes, stir-fry until onions are golden. Remove the pan from the heat, stir-in the yoghurt mixed with coriander, red chilli and turmeric powders. Return the pan to the heat and stir-fry till specks of fat begin to appear on the surface.

Add tomato purée and potatoes, and stir-fry until fat leaves the sides. Add about 4 cups of water and salt and bring to the boil; reduce heat to low and simmer, stirring occasionally, until potatoes are three-fourth cooked.

Add the drained *vadi* and bring to the boil. Reduce heat to low heat and simmer, stirring occasionally, until the potatoes are cooked and the gravy is of a thin sauce-like consistency. Sprinkle dry fenugreek leaf powder and stir. Remove and adjust the seasoning. Transfer to a serving dish, garnish with green coriander and serve with chapatti.

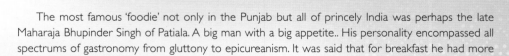

The most famous 'foodie' not only in the Punjab but all of princely India was perhaps the late Maharaja Bhupinder Singh of Patiala. A big man with a big appetite.. His personality encompassed all spectrums of gastronomy from gluttony to epicureanism. It was said that for breakfast he had more

BOTTLE GOURD KOFTAS STUFFED WITH DRIED PLUMS IN THICK GRAVY

INGREDIENTS

Bottle gourd (*lauki*), peeled, grated	500 gm / 1.1 lb
Gram flour (*besan*)	100 gm / 3½ oz
Green chillies, deseeded, finely chopped	2
Ginger (*adrak*), finely chopped	10 gm / 1" piece
Black pepper (*kaali mirch*), freshly roasted, coarsely ground	½ tsp / 1½ gm
Salt to taste	
Dried plums (*alubukhara*), pit removed and stuffed with almond	16
Vegetable oil for deep-frying the koftas	

For the gravy:

Ghee	¼ cup / 60 gm / 2 oz
Green cardamom (*choti elaichi*)	3
Cloves (*laung*)	2
Cinnamon (*dalchini*), 1" stick	1
Bay leaf (*tej patta*)	1
Onions, grated	100 gm / 3½ oz
Garlic (*lasan*) paste	3¼ tsp / 20 gm
Ginger paste	2½ tsp / 15 gm
Coriander (*dhaniya*) powder	1 tbsp / 9 gm
Red chilli powder	1 tsp / 3 gm
Turmeric (*haldi*) powder	½ tsp / 1½ gm
Tomato purée, fresh	3 cups / 720 gm
Salt to taste	
Black cardamom (*moti elaichi*) powder	½ tsp / 1½ gm
Dry fenugreek leaf (*kasoori methi*) powder	a pinch
Green coriander (*hara dhaniya*), chopped	1 tbsp / 4 gm

METHOD

Boil the bottle gourd with a little salt until cooked. Drain and then squeeze in a napkin to ensure it is completely devoid of moisture.

Mix gram flour, green chillies, ginger, black pepper, and salt with the bottle gourd; knead well. Divide into 16 equal portions. Flatten each portion between the palms, place a stuffed plum in the middle and reshape into balls again. Deep-fry the koftas on medium heat in hot oil until golden brown. Remove and drain the excess oil on absorbent paper towels.

For the gravy:

Heat the ghee in a pan; add green cardamom, cloves, cinnamon stick, and bay leaves, stir on medium heat until cardamom begins to change colour. Add onions and sauté until translucent and glossy. Add ginger and garlic pastes, and sauté until onions become light pink. Add the spice powders dissolved in 3 tbsp water, and stir-fry until the moisture evaporates. Add tomato purée, stir-fry until specks of fat begin to appear on the surface. Add approximately 1 cup of water, bring to the boil. Reduce heat to low and simmer, stirring occasionally for 2-3 minutes. Add fried koftas and simmer for 2 minutes. Mix in the remaining ingredients. Serve hot.

than two-dozen eggs and routinely demolished half a dozen chicken. There was substantial nourishment at other meals too. All his appetites were voracious. His nocturnal exertions, he thought, required extra dietary supplements and his interest in matters culinary was strongly tinged with a love for aphrodisiacs. *Piste ka salan* is believed to have been revived by the Awadhi cooks at his instance. He was a lavish host and arguably, after Maharaja Ranjit Singh, the first Sikh ruler to have employed foreign cooks and encouraged fusion in the kitchen.

Facing page: Maharaja Bhupinder Singh

MAKKI KI ROTI

SERVES: 4

MAIZE FLOUR BREAD

INGREDIENTS

Maize flour (*makki ka atta*)	500 gm / 1.1 lb
Salt to taste	
Water as required	
Butter, melted	1/2 cup / 100 gm / 3 1/2 oz

METHOD

Sieve the maize flour with salt. Make a bay, pour water in it and start mixing gradually. When fully mixed, knead to make a soft dough. Cover with a moist cloth and keep aside for 30 minutes.

Divide the dough equally into 8 portions, make balls and cover them for 5 minutes.

Flatten each ball between the palms to make a round disc, place the roti on a cushioned pad (*gaddi*) and stick inside a tandoor. Bake for 2 minutes. Apply melted butter. Repeat till all are baked. Serve hot.

SARSON KA SAAG

SERVES: 4

MUSTARD GREENS

INGREDIENTS

Mustard leaves (*sarson ka saag*), roughly chopped	750 gm / 1 lb 11 oz
Spinach (*palak*), roughly chopped	250 gm / 9 oz
White radish leaves (*mooli patta*), roughly chopped	100 gm / 3 1/2 oz
Bathua, roughly chopped	30 gm / 1 oz
Ginger (*adrak*), diced	3" piece / 30 gm
Green chillies, slit, deseeded	8
Rice	45 gm / 1 1/2 oz
Mustard (*sarson*) oil	1/4 cup / 60 ml / 2 fl oz
Salt to taste	
Maize flour (*makki ka atta*)	15 gm / 1/2 oz
White butter	1 cup / 200 gm / 7 oz

METHOD

Combine all the ingredients together (except maize flour and white butter) in a pan. Add 8 cups of water and bring to the boil. Reduce heat to low and simmer for approximately 1.45 hours or until the greens are tender.

Remove the pan from the heat and churn with a wooden churner (*madhani*). Return the pan to the heat, add maize flour, cover and simmer on very low heat, stirring at regular intervals, for 1 hour. Remove and adjust the seasoning. Transfer to a bowl, garnish with large dollops of butter and serve with *makki ki roti*.

Heading towards Delhi the traveller on the GT road reaches Karnal and Panipat next. Kurukshetra, the mythological battleground made famous by the Hindu epic the *Mahabharata*, is bypassed without much fuss. The township of Karnal commemorates the ill-fated warrior Karna whose rivalry with Arjuna provides great dramatic tension in that epic. The town is mid-way (roughly) between Delhi and Chandigarh and is the favourite rest stop of travellers on this route. A number of *dhabas* and fast-food joints have sprouted here on both sides of the Grand Trunk Road.

Facing page: The exuberant *bhangra* is a dance celebrating the Punjabi *joi de vivre*, a must at the harvest festival.

Alternatively one can opt for the R&R at Panipat that has been the battlefield of three major encounters that have changed the course of Indian history. Babur, the first victor, went on to claim the throne of Delhi ousting the Lodi Sultans. Akbar, his grandson, proved his mettle by quelling the revolt of Hemu to assert his sovereign power and when Ahmed Shah Abdali routed the Marathas he opened the floodgates of chaos and anarchy preparing the ground for the British takeover in future. Today, a simple plaque standing amidst verdant fields marks the once blood-soaked battlefield bearing mute testimony to those tumultuous events. This tract of land forms part of the state of Haryana that was

The hard work over it is time for playing hard. Robust repast accompanies both activities.

VEGETABLE STUFFED BAKED BREAD

INGREDIENTS

For the dough:

Refined flour (*maida*), sieved	400 gm / 14 oz
Salt	a pinch
Water	3 cups / 750 ml / 24 fl oz
Ghee	½ cup / 100 gm / 3½ oz

For the filling:

Potatoes, boiled, peeled, grated	175 gm / 6 oz
Cauliflower (*phool gobi*), washed, grated	150 gm / 5 oz
Cottage cheese (*paneer*), grated	35 gm / 1¼ oz
Ginger (*adrak*), finely chopped	2 tsp / 6 gm
Green coriander (*hara dhaniya*), finely chopped	1 tbsp / 4 gm
Green chillies, deseeded, chopped	1 tbsp
Onion, finely chopped	¼ cup / 35 gm / 1 oz
Black pepper (*kaali mirch*) powder	1 tsp / 3 gm
Dried pomegranate seed (*anaar dana*) powder	1 tsp / 3 gm
Cumin (*jeera*) seeds	1 tsp / 2 gm
Carom (*ajwain*) seeds	1 tsp / 2½ gm
Coriander (*dhaniya*) seeds, freshly broiled, crushed	1 tsp / 2 gm
Dry fenugreek leaf (*kasoori methi*) powder	1 tsp
Garam masala powder	1 tsp / 3 gm

METHOD

For the filling:

Mix all the ingredients in a bowl. Divide into 8 equal portions.

For the dough:

Make a bay in the sieved flour, pour water in it and start mixing gradually. When fully mixed knead to make a soft but smooth dough. Cover with a moist cloth and keep aside for 30 minutes. Add half the ghee, knead and punch the dough. Cover with a moist cloth and keep aside for another 10 minutes. Divide into 8 equal portions; make balls and place on a lightly floured surface. Cover yet again with a moist cloth and keep aside for 5 minutes.

Place the balls on a lightly floured surface and flatten each with a rolling pin into round discs (approximately 4″ diameter). Place a portion of the filling in the middle, enfold the filling and pinch off the excess dough to seal the edges. Then flatten again with a rolling pin.

Place the round disc on a cushioned pad (*gaddi*), stick inside a moderately hot tandoor and bake for 3-4 minutes. Alternatively, in the pre-heated oven, place on a greased baking tray and bake for 10 minutes. Apply ghee on the *kulcha* as soon as it is removed from the tandoor or oven and serve immediately.

carved out of Punjab about four decades back and is known as the 'bread basket' of India. Home to the rustic Jats and Yadavas, the land is predominantly vegetarian. This is where you can indulge in *karhi pakora, dal tarka, mattar paneer, aloo palak, palak paneer* and a variety of fresh seasonal vegetables to your heart's content. A large plate of green salad with a bowl full of *dahi* or *raita* is the usual welcome accompaniment. The *dhabas* on the roadside are usually found in clusters and present the look of crowded fair grounds. The names of the dishes may sound similar to those served in Punjab but by the time a distance of 350 odd km is traversed from Amritsar, the palate can easily register the difference in taste. Sometimes it is the tempering, at others, avoidance of onion and garlic. Even the ghee used has a different fragrance.

PASANDA KEBAB

SKEWERED LAMB STEAKS

INGREDIENTS

Lamb boneless, steak		Egg white	I
cleaned, pat-dried	1200 gm	Cream	1½ cups / 300 ml / 11 fl oz
For the first marinade:		Cashew nut (*kaju*)	
Raw papaya paste		paste	5 tbsp / 75 gm / 2½ oz
for tenderizing	3" piece	White pepper powder	½ tbsp / 4½ gm
Salt to taste		Green cardamom	
White pepper		(*choti elaichi*) powder	½ tsp / 1½ gm
(*safed mirch*) powder	I tsp / 3 gm	Allspice (*kebabchini*) powder	½ tsp
Ginger-garlic		Green chillies, deseeded, chopped	20 gm
(*adrak-lasan*) paste	I tbsp / 18 gm		
For the second marinade:		Melted butter for basting	
Cottage cheese (*paneer*),			
grated	150 gm / 5 oz		

METHOD

For the first marinade:
Mix all the ingredients and apply over the lamb; keep aside for 1 hour.

For the second marinade:
In a deep tray, mix the cottage cheese with the egg white with your palm. Add cream gradually and mix until well blended. Add cashew nut paste and all the remaining ingredients.

Marinate the lamb in the seconde marinade and keep aside for 2-3 hours.

Take a skewer, skew the marinated lamb, one by one, and roast in preheated tandoor or over charcoal grill for about 8-10 minutes. Remove and hang so that the excess moisture drains out completely (1-2 minutes). Baste with melted butter and further roast for about 3-5 minutes. Remove and serve hot along with choice of salad or chutney.

It was the Urdu poet Zauk who famously remarked, '*Kaun jaye Zauk yeh Dilli ki galiyaan chod kar,*' (Tell me why one should ever think of bidding adieu to the charming streets of Delhi?). One can easily understand his reluctance to step out of the city. Street foods here have always been enticing. Denizens of Delhi have a reputation of being great droolers who can never resist a delicious temptation. They were called *chatoras* (those who could not resist any delicious temptation and were obsessive tasters). The average Delhiite spent lavishly on hospitality.

Facing page: Chandni Chowk, the street of silversmiths, the heart of old city.

ISHTEW

LAMB STEW

INGREDIENTS

Lamb (chops and pieces from shoulder)	800 gm / 28 oz
Vegetable oil	½ cup / 120 ml / 4 fl oz
Onions, medium-sized, sliced	500 gm / 1.1 lb
Ginger (adrak), roughly chopped	3" piece
Garlic (lasan) flakes	15-18
Black peppercorns (sabut kaali mirch)	1 tsp / 4 gm
Dry red chillies (sookhi lal mirch)	6-8
Turmeric (haldi), coarsely pounded	1" piece
Yoghurt (dahi)	1 cup / 250 gm / 9 oz
Salt to taste	
Green chillies, slit	2-3

METHOD

Heat the oil in a thick-bottomed pan; add the meat, onions, ginger, garlic, black peppercorns, dry red chillies, and turmeric.

Whisk the yoghurt and pour into the pan. Sprinkle salt and cook covered on low-medium heat, stirring at regular intervals. Do not add any water. When the meat is done to taste remove and serve hot garnished with green chillies.

PAPRI CHAAT

SAVOURY BISCUITS WITH YOGHURT

INGREDIENTS

For the papri:

Refined flour (maida)	250 gm / 9 oz
Salt	½ tsp / 1½ gm
Cumin (jeera) seeds	½ tsp / 1 gm
Cold water	6-8 tbsp / 90-120 ml / 2-4 fl oz
Ghee, melted	2 tbsp / 30 gm / 1 oz
Ghee for frying	2½ cups / 500 gm / 1.1 lb

For the yoghurt:

Yoghurt (dahi), whipped	2 cups / 500 gm / 1.1 lb
Salt	1½ tsp / 4½ gm
Cumin seeds, roasted, powdered	2-3 tsp / 4-6 gm
Red chilli powder	1 tsp / 3 gm
Tamarind chutney (meethi sonth), see facing page for recipe	

METHOD

For the papri:

Sieve the flour and salt together. Add cumin seeds and enough cold water to make stiff dough. Knead thoroughly, adding melted ghee. Roll out thinly and cut out discs ½" in diameter. Prick the discs with a fork.

Heat the ghee in a wok (kadhai); fry the discs, a few at a time, till golden. Remove, drain and keep aside.

For the yoghurt:

Mix the yoghurt with salt and cumin powder. Arrange the discs on a platter; pour yoghurt and tamarind chutney on top. Sprinkle with cumin, red chilli powders, and chaat masala.

The city, the threshold to the heartland of India, is believed to have had seven incarnations. It started as Dillika or Rai Pithora in the days of the Chavanas circa twelfth century. Siri was the second, a prosperous city built by Allauddin Khilji in 1303. Tughlaqabad was built as a dramatic fort city by Ghiyasuddin Tughlaq but never flourished as his nephew Muhammad Tughlaq built his own capital at Jahanpanah between Siri and Rai Pithora. His successor Feroze Shah Tughlaq was no less ambitious and founded Ferozabad. This site is marked by the sprawling ruins of Feroze Shah Kotla. Sher Shah Suri built the Purana Qila. The latest in this line is Shahjahanabad, the city so lovingly raised by the builder of the Taj Mahal. The British after moving the imperial capital from Calcutta to Delhi held a glittering Imperial

ALOO CHAAT

SERVES: 4

HOT 'N' SWEET POTATOES

INGREDIENTS

Potatoes, boiled, peeled,	
cut into 1/2" cubes	600 gm / 22 oz
Vegetable oil	5 tsp / 25 ml
Tamarind chutney	
(*meethi sonth*)	90 gm / 3 oz
Onion, chopped	2 tbsp / 20 gm
Ginger (*adrak*), chopped	1½ tsp / 10 gm
Green coriander (*hara dhaniya*),	
chopped	2½ tbsp / 10 gm
Green chillies, deseeded,	
chopped	1 tbsp / 5 gm
Red chilli powder	1½ tsp / 5 gm
Chaat masala	2½ tsp / 8 gm
Salt	1 tsp / 3 gm
Lemon (*nimbu*) juice	2 tbsp / 30 ml / 1 fl oz

METHOD

Heat the oil in a pan; sauté the potatoes for a minute on medium heat. Cool add the remaining ingredients and toss gently (to ensure that the potatoes do not get mashed).

Arrange equal portions of the potatoes in 4 serving dishes and garnish with chopped tomatoes and lemon wedges.

MEETHI SONTH

MAKES: 2 CUPS

SWEET AND SOUR TAMARIND CHUTNEY

INGREDIENTS

Tamarind (*imli*)	150 gm / 5 oz
Jaggery	3-4 tbsps / 9-12 gm
Ginger powder (*sonth*)	1 tsp / 3 gm
Cumin (*jeera*) seeds,	
roasted, powdered	1 tsp / 2 gm
Salt	2 tsp / 6 gm
Red chilli powder	1/2 tsp / 1½ gm

METHOD

Soak the tamarind in 3 cups of hot water for 1-2 hours. Pass through a sieve, squeezing out all the pulp.

Mix in the remaining ingredients and stir well to dissolve the jaggery. Adjust seasoning to taste and add a little water if the chutney is too thick. Chill and use as required.

Durbar here and unveiled their plans to build a capital to match the majesty of their empire. This is the New Delhi that Edward Lutyens planned and built. There are many a majestic monuments that identify Delhi—the Qutab Minar, Red Fort, Jama Masjid, Jantar Mantar, India Gate, and Rashtrapati Bhawan. These buildings are like interesting chapters in the biography of this historic city spanning a period of over eight-hundred years. They bear testimony to the artistic genius and creativity of the master craftsmen who dwelt here.

A contemporary *chaatwalla*. His apron announcing that he is keeping up with changing trends.

Food Path: Cuisine along the Grand Trunk Road

DAHI KI GUJIYA

STUFFED BLACK GRAM FRITTERS IN YOGHURT

INGREDIENTS

For the *gujiya*:

Husked black beans (*dhuli urad dal*), soaked in cold water for 8-10 hours	1¼ cups / 250 gm / 9 oz
Soda bicarbonate	½ tsp
Asafoetida (*hing*)	a pinch
Ginger (*adrak*), finely chopped	2" piece
Green chillies, finely chopped	1-2
Mint (*pudina*) leaves, finely chopped	2 tsp
Raisins (*kishmish*)	2 tbsp / 25 gm
Ghee for frying	2½ cups / 500 gm / 1.1 lb

For the yoghurt:

Yoghurt (*dahi*), whipped	2 cups / 500 gm / 1.1 lb
Cumin (*jeera*) seeds, roasted, ground	2 tsp / 4 gm
Red chilli powder	¼ tsp
Salt	1 tsp / 3 gm

METHOD

For the *gujiya*:

Drain and grind the black gram to a fine paste. Mix in sodium bicarbonate and asafoetida and whip the mixture till fluffy.

Mix together ginger, green chillies, mint, and raisins and keep aside.

Heat the ghee in a wok (*kadhai*); stretch a moistened piece of muslin over the rim of a glass. Using wet hands make small balls of mixture and flatten lightly on the muslin. Put a small amount of ginger mixture in the centre and fold over to make a semi-circle, using the muslin to aid you. Gently press the edges to enclose the filling. Test if ghee is hot enough by putting a small amount of dal paste into the wok it should float to the surface almost immediately. Using a wet knife slide the *gujiya* carefully into the hot ghee and fry till pale gold. Repeat till all are fried. Put the fried *gujiyas* into a bowl of warm, salted water and leave for 10 minutes.

For the yoghurt:

Mix the yoghurt with cumin and red chilli powders, and salt. Gently squeeze the *gujiyas* to extract the excess water and arrange in a shallow dish. Pour seasoned yoghurt over the *gujiyas*. Serve chilled garnished with cumin and red chilli powders.

The Nai Sarak in old Delhi is where, arguably, the best *chaat* is served. *Chaat* comprises assorted savouries, *tikkis*, *papri*, *golgappe*, fruits dished out with sweet and sour chutneys or fresh fruits drizzled with tangy sprinklers for snacking between meals. The *chaat* seller carries this moveable feast with him on a *khomcha*, a shoulder held portable stall made of bamboo reeds on which the flat griddle can be balanced and an assortment of savouries served. Women from respectable families were not expected to step out and eat on the streets. The *khomchawala* would bring the movable feast to their doorstep. This was fast food, Indian style. The patron could adjust the spicing according to the taste and the whim of the moment. The standard fare has remained unchanged.

STUFFED OKRA

INGREDIENTS

Okra (*bhindi*), small, caps
    and tips sliced off, slit   600 gm / 22 oz

For the filling:

Ghee   2 tbsp / 30 gm / 1 oz

Mango powder (*amchur*)   1 tbsp / 9 gm

Coriander (*dhaniya*) powder   1¹/₂ tsp / 4¹/₂ gm

Fennel (*saunf*) powder   1¹/₂ tsp / 4¹/₂ gm

Cumin (*jeera*) powder   1 tsp / 3 gm

Black pepper (*kaali mirch*),
    freshly roasted, coarsely ground   1 tsp / 3 gm

Red chilli powder   1 tsp / 3 gm

Turmeric (*haldi*) powder   1 tsp / 3 gm

Black cardamom
    (*moti elaichi*) powder   ¹/₂ tsp / 1¹/₂ gm

Nutmeg (*jaiphal*) powder   ¹/₄ tsp

Salt to taste

For the gravy:

Ghee   ¹/₄ cup / 50 gm / 1³/₄ oz

Onions, sliced   150 gm / 5 oz

Red chilli powder   1 tsp / 3 gm

Turmeric (*haldi*) powder   ¹/₂ tsp / 1¹/₂ gm

Yoghurt (*dahi*), whisked   3 cups / 720 ml / 27 oz

Salt to taste

For the garnish:

Dry red chillies, deseeded, cut into juliennes

Ginger, cut into juliennes and reserved
    in lemon juice

METHOD

For the filling:

Mix all the ingredients in a bowl. Pack the okra with equal quantities of the filling.

For the gravy:

Heat the ghee in a wok (*kadhai*); add onions and sauté on low heat until translucent and glossy (ensure that the onions do not get coloured). Add red chilli and turmeric powders (dissolved in 2 tbsp of water); stir-fry until the moisture evaporates.

Add the stuffed okra, cover and cook on medium heat, stirring occasionally, for 7-8 minutes. Remove the wok from the heat, stir-in yoghurt and salt. Return the wok to the heat and cook, stirring occasionally, but carefully (to ensure that the filling does not ooze out completely), until of custard consistency. Remove and adjust the seasoning.

Serve hot garnished with dry red chillies and ginger juliennes.

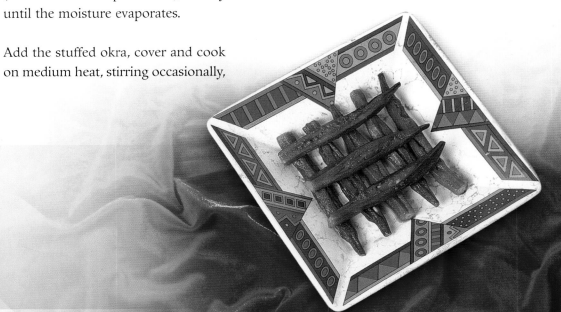

On the other side, stands the Kashmiri Gate where there is a specialized market of auto parts and the Interstate Bus Terminal. This is where one can sample the vanishing delicacy: *berhvin* with *methi ki chutney* or *kachoris* with *sitaphal ki subzi*. Vegetarian fare usually served at the roadside *dhaba* on the Grand Trunk Road lacks variety so make the most of these meals before you hit the good old road again.

It is easy to overlook that the food in this city is as resplendent and as exciting as its majestic monuments. Many distinct culinary streams mingle here and have harmoniously coexisted for generations, the Muslim-Turko, Afghan and the Mughals, Hindu-Bania, Kayastha and Punjabi. Eateries like Karim in the Walled City trace their ancestry to the days of Shah Jahan. Even those who do not boast

SUBZION KI TAHAREE

VEGETABLE PULAO

INGREDIENTS

Basmati rice, picked, washed, drained	1½ cups / 300 gm / 11 oz

For the bouquet garni: Pounded in a mortar and pestal and tied in muslin cloth:

Black peppercorns (sabut kaali mirch)	12
Fennel (saunf) seeds	2 tsp / 5 gm
Green cardamom (choti elaichi)	5
Black cardamom (moti elaichi)	4
Cloves (laung)	4
Bay leaves (tej patta)	2
Cinnamon (dalchini), 1" sticks	2

For the vegetables:

Potatoes, medium-sized, quartered	6
Cauliflower (phool gobi)	110 gm / 3½ oz
Carrots (gajar)	110 gm / 3½ oz
Green peas (hara mattar)	60 gm / 2 oz
Ghee	4 tbsp / 60 gm / 2 oz
Green cardamom	4
Cloves	3
Cinnamon, 1" stick	1
Ginger (adrak) paste	5 tsp / 30 gm / 1 oz
Garlic (lasan) paste	2½ tsp / 15 gm
Onions, fried till light golden	110 gm / 3½ oz
Red chilli powder	1 tsp / 3 gm
Turmeric (haldi) powder	½ tsp / 1½ gm
Water	4 cups / 1 lt / 4 pints
Salt to taste	
Tomatoes, large, coarsely chopped	3
Green coriander (hara dhaniya), coarsely chopped	1½ tbsp / 6 gm
Mint (pudina) leaves, coarsely chopped	1 tbsp / 2 gm
Green chillies, chopped	4
Lemon (nimbu) juice	1 tbsp / 15 ml

METHOD

Add the bouquet garni in the rice and reserve for 45 minutes.

Boil the potatoes with enough water to cover; adding a pinch of salt, turmeric and yellow chilli powders. Boil until half cooked, drain and pat dry. Blanch the cauliflower and carrots in salted boiling water for a minute, drain and refresh in iced water.

Heat the ghee in a pan; add the whole garam masala and stir on medium heat until cardamom changes colour. Reduce heat to medium-low, add the ginger and garlic pastes, and stir until the moisture evaporates. Add the blanched vegetables, stir for a minute. Add fried onions, and stir-fry for a couple of minutes. Add the red chilli and turmeric powders (dissolved in 2 tbsp of water), stir. Add water and bring to the boil. Reduce heat to low, add tomatoes, green coriander, mint, and green chillies; stir. Add rice with the bouquet garni, stir and bring to the boil. Add salt and lemon juice; stir, cover and simmer (without stirring) until the rice is cooked and the stock is fully absorbed. Remove, discard the bouquet garni and serve with *raita*.

of such a noble lineage, like Jawahar and New Jawahar, treat their guests with resplendent fare. There are certain delicacies that are quintessentially Delhi fare—*ishtew, pasande* and *nihari*. The eateries in Old Delhi usually eschew the tandoor as the patrons prefer the *khameeri* and *roomali* over the *tandoori roti. Kheer* that is ubiquitous in Punjab and Haryana is gently replaced by the soufflé like *phirni* and *kulfi*, the Indian ice cream created to please the palate of Akbar the Great, makes a dramatic appearance. No exploration of taste in Shahjehanabad can be complete without a visit to the Moti Mahal in Daryaganj, the restaurant that in the 1950's made the tandoori chicken world famous.

Facing page: Bird's eyeview of the breathtaking vista from the minaret of the grand Jama Masjid.

GOBI KA PARATHA

CAULIFLOWER STUFFED UNLEAVENED BREAD

INGREDIENTS

Wholewheat flour (*atta*)
dough   3¹⁄₃ cups / 500 gm / 1.1 lb
Butter   ³⁄₄ cup / 150 gm / 5 oz
Wholewheat flour for dusting

For the filling:

Cauliflower (*phool gobi*),
washed, grated   250 gm / 9 oz
Green chillies, chopped   1 tbsp / 5 gm
Green coriander (*hara dhaniya*),
chopped   2¹⁄₂ tbsp / 10 gm
Cumin (*jeera*) seeds,
roasted, powdered   2 tsp / 5 gm
Salt to taste

METHOD

For the filling:

Mix all the ingredients and keep aside.

Divide the dough into 8 equal portions and shape each portion into a ball. Flatten the balls on a lightly floured surface with a rolling pin into a round disc approximately 6″ in diameter.

Take two round discs at a time. Spread a portion of the filling in middle of one disc. Place the second disc on top and seal from the sides with the help of fingers. Flatten again with a rolling pin approximately 7″ in diameter.

Heat the griddle (*tawa*); half bake the parathas, turning over once. For each melt 40 gm of butter and shallow-fry until golden brown on both sides. Remove and repeat till all are fried.

Serve immediately with pickle and yoghurt.

Remnants of a tandoor (clay oven) have been discovered from an excavation at the Indus Valley sites. Its proliferation and popularity though should be credited to the intrepid and extremely mobile Punjabi. The credit for making tandoori delicacies world famous is due to Sri Kundan Lal, founder of the legendary Moti Mahal restaurant in Old Delhi. This eatery became popular with the Capital's elite in the 1950's. Today, the boneless *tikka* culled from chicken breast is more popular than the whole bird and in its chicken tikka masala avatar has established itself as the National Dish of Great Britain.

Qutab Minar built by Qutubuddin Aibak of the Slave dynasty.

ALOO KA PARATHA

POTATO STUFFED UNLEAVENED BREAD

INGREDIENTS

Wholewheat flour (*atta*)
for the dough   3¹/₃ cups / 500 gm / 1.1 lb

Butter   ³/₄ cup / 150 gm / 5 oz

Wholewheat flour for dusting

For the filling:

Potatoes, boiled, grated   150 gm / 5 oz

Ginger (*adrak*), chopped   1 tbsp / 20 gm

Green chillies, chopped   1 tbsp / 5 gm

Green coriander (*hara dhaniya*),
chopped   2¹/₂ tbsp / 10 gm

Pomegranate seeds
(*anaar dana*)   1 tsp / 3 gm

Red chilli powder   1¹/₂ tsp / 5 gm

Salt to taste

METHOD

For the filling:
Mix all the ingredients together and keep aside.

Divide the dough into 8 equal portions and shape each portion into a ball. Flatten the balls on a lightly floured surface with a rolling pin into a round disc approximately 6" in diameter.

Take two round discs at a time. Spread a portion of the filling in middle of one disc. Place the second disc on top and seal from the sides with the help of fingers. Flatten again with a rolling pin approximately 7" in diameter.

Heat a griddle (*tawa*), half bake the parathas, turning over once. For each melt 40 gm of butter and shallow-fry until golden brown on both sides. Remove and repeat with the other dough.

Serve immediately with pickle and yoghurt.

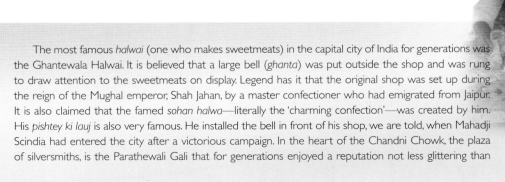

The most famous *halwai* (one who makes sweetmeats) in the capital city of India for generations was the Ghantewala Halwai. It is believed that a large bell (*ghanta*) was put outside the shop and was rung to draw attention to the sweetmeats on display. Legend has it that the original shop was set up during the reign of the Mughal emperor, Shah Jahan, by a master confectioner who had emigrated from Jaipur. It is also claimed that the famed *sohan halwa*—literally the 'charming confection'—was created by him. His *pishtey ki lauj* is also very famous. He installed the bell in front of his shop, we are told, when Mahadji Scindia had entered the city after a victorious campaign. In the heart of the Chandni Chowk, the plaza of silversmiths, is the Parathewali Gali that for generations enjoyed a reputation not less glittering than

BERHVIN PURI

DEEP-FRIED BREAD STUFFED WITH BLACK GRAM

INGREDIENTS

For the dough:

Whole wheat flour (*atta*)	500 gm / 1.1 lb
Salt	a pinch

For the stuffing:

Husked black gram (*dhuli urad dal*), soaked for 8-10 hours	2/3 cup / 125 gm / 4 oz
Ginger (*adrak*), finely chopped	2 tsp / 12 gm
Coriander (*dhaniya*) seeds, crushed	3 tsp / 6 gm
Aniseed (*saunf*)	1 tsp / 2 gm
Red chilli powder	1/2 tsp / 1 1/2 gm
Green coriander (*hara dhaniya*), chopped	2 tsp
Ghee for frying	2 1/2 cups / 500 gm / 1.1 lb

METHOD

For the dough:

Sieve the whole wheat flour with salt and make a bay in the centre, pour water and knead to make a dough. Cover with a moist cloth and keep aside for 30 minutes. Divide the dough into 20 equal portions and shape into balls. Apply a little oil, cover with a wet cloth, and keep aside.

For the stuffing:

Drain the black gram and grind to a fine, fairly stiff paste. Mix in the remaining ingredients (except ghee). Put 1 tsp of the filling in the centre of the ball and fold over to enclose the filling completely. Roll out into round discs of 4″ diameter.

Heat the ghee in a wok (*kadhai*); fry the stuffed puris, in small batches, till golden brown on both sides. Remove and drain the excess oil on absorbent paper towels. Serve hot.

that of the jewellers in its neighbourhood. The Parathewali Gali in Delhi, today, alas, has lost its lustre but superb parathas can still be enjoyed in Agra.

Facing page: The congregation of the faithful performing *namaaz* at the Jama Masjid, Delhi, the largest mosque in Asia.

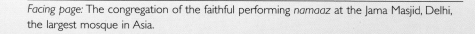

DRY VERMICELLI FLAVOURED WITH SCREWPINE ESSENCE

INGREDIENTS

Vermicelli (*sev*), fine	250 gm / 9 oz
Ghee	1¼ cups / 250 gm / 9 oz
Milk	2 cups / 500 ml / 16 fl oz
Sugar	2½ cups / 500 gm / 1.1 lb
Screwpine (*kewra*) essence	2-3 drops
Wholemilk fudge (*khoya*), crumbled or	
grated	1¼ cups / 250 gm / 9 oz
Almonds (*badaam*), sliced	20 / 25 gm

METHOD

Heat the ghee in a wok (*kadhai*); fry the vermicelli in 5-6 batches, till light brown. (If you are using pre-roasted vermicelli, fry each batch for 1-2 minutes.) Remove and drain the vermicelli on absorbent kitchen paper towels.

Bring the milk to the boil in a pot. Remove and add fried vermicelli. Press gently with a spoon so that all the vermicelli is moistened. Cover and leave to soak for 10 minutes.

Melt the sugar in a separate pan with ½ cup of water, stirring on gentle heat until the sugar dissolves completely, then boil rapidly for one minute.

Pour the sugar syrup in the vermicelli and milk mixture and return the pan to very gentle heat. Cover and cook undisturbed for 15-20 minutes or till the liquid has been absorbed. Each strand of vermicelli should be separate. Add screwpine essence and wholemilk fudge and turn with a fork to mix.

Transfer into a dish and serve chilled garnished with almonds.

The Mughals while travelling eastwards took the scenic route through Agra but unfortunately the present day Grand Trunk Road bypasses it and swings away via Aligarh to Etawa and to Kanpur. However, Mathura, touched by the historic highway, does provide an opportunity to digress a little to visit the Taj and the Fatehpuri Sikri complex. The *peda* from Mathura, the historic city associated with the pranks and heroism of the playful dark god Sri Krishna, can be tried out when the journey is resumed.

Noor Jahan and Jahangir on the facing page. Lovers of good life, the couple travelled frequently on the Grand Trunk Road and patronized master chefs.

NIMISH

INDIAN SOUFFLÉ

INGREDIENTS

Full-cream milk, unboiled	8 cups / 2 lt / 4 pints
Cream	2 cups / 500 gm / 1.1 lb
Cream of tartar	1 tsp
Caster sugar	1 cup / 200 gm / 7 oz
Rose water (*gulaab jal*)	1 tsp / 5 ml
Pistachios (*pista*), finely sliced	2 tbsp / 25 gm

METHOD

Combine the milk, cream, and cream of tartar in a large bowl and refrigerate overnight.

Next morning stir in 4 tsp caster sugar and rose water and whisk the mixture using a rotary or electric beater at high speed. Using a tea strainer collect the foam that forms and transfer to a large tray. Keep the tray tilted so that the foam stays on one side; some milk will collect on the lower side. When the tray is fairly full, spoon the foam into clay saucers or teacups, sprinkling a little caster sugar between layers and on top. (The foam will condense a little during this operation. What looks like four bowlfuls in the tray will yield only two bowls.) Pour the milk collected in the tray back into the bowl and continue beating and collecting the foam till all the milk is used up. The whole process will take 2-2½ hours.

Sprinkle pistachios on top of each bowl of foam and refrigerate till serving time.

The mouthwatering temptations in Agra are the out-of-this-world parathas served at Rambabu Paratha Bhandar and the puris at Chimanlal near the cantonment railway station. Here in Belanganj, the street of the rolling pin,, a titanic paratha is first baked, then fried on a huge griddle weighing more than 30 kg. A single paratha with accompaniments can serve as a full meal for a small family.

Agra is synonymous with Taj Mahal and *petha*, an unusual sweet, with the look and the texture of candied fruit. The plain Jane *petha* is sold dry or in syrup but there are many other seductive varieties: *anguri*, chiseled like grapes or the saffron-tinged *kesaria*. The *petha* travels well due to its long shelf life.

KULFI

FROZEN MILK DESSERT

INGREDIENTS

Full-cream milk	8 cups / 2 lt / 8 pints
Sugar	³/₄ cup / 150 gm / 5 oz
Almonds (*badaam*),	
blanched and ground	40 / 50 gm
Screwpine (*kewra*) essence	a few drops
Metal *kulfi* moulds, washed and dried	

METHOD

Bring the milk to the boil in a large pan. Reduce heat and continue to cook, stirring from time to time till the milk has reduced to a little less than half the original volume. This will take 30-40 minutes.

Remove from heat, add sugar and stir to dissolve. Stir in almonds and screwpine essence. Cool the mixture, then pour into *kulfi* moulds leaving 1" space at the top for the *kulfi* to expand. Cover firmly with lids and deep-freeze for 8-10 hours or till frozen.

To serve, roll the mould in your hands, run a sharp knife around inside the edge and unmould onto a plate.

Note: The Mughals developed this frozen milk dessert in Delhi. They brought ice to Delhi from a mountain near Kasauli called Choori Chandni ka Dhar which is perennially covered with snow. Abul Fazl tells us that salt peter for cooling was introduced in India by Akbar. The method of making *kulfi* has remained unchanged to the present day.

Thickened milk is put into special conical moulds and frozen by putting these in a large pot filled with a mixture of ice and salt, which is shaken gently till the *kulfi* freezes. The moulds can be of metal, but the traditional earthenware moulds give a lovely flavour to the *kulfi*. A *baraf ki handi* (a pot full of *kulfi*) is a very special gift to send someone.

The ride on this stretch of the Grand Trunk Road begins to get bumpier. The ambitious Golden Quadrilateral dream of upgrading the national highways is yet to be realized and driving on narrow single lanes can be quite scary. Small towns like Ferozabad, celebrated for its delicate glass bangles and Khurja, famous for its pottery, whiz past as cars, trucks and buses try to speed away regardless of the increasing congestion and unruly traffic of tractors, trolleys, bullock carts, 'make do' *jugads* and reckless tempo drivers. Occasionally a suicidal cyclist or scooterist swerves in and out to enliven the proceedings. It is a relief to reach Aligarh.

Facing page: Taj Mahal, the mausoleum in marble that immortalizes Shah Jahan's love for Mumtaz Mahal.

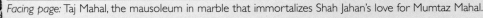

BOTI KEBAB

GRILLED LAMB CHUNKS

INGREDIENTS

Lamb chunks (*boti*), washed,
pat-dried   I kg / 20 pieces

For the first marinade:

Raw papaya paste for tenderizing	4" × 4"
Ginger-garlic (*adrak-lasan*) paste	I tbsp / 18 gm
Red chilli paste	I tbsp / 15 gm
Salt to taste	
Vinegar (*sirka*)	4 tsp / 20 ml
Vegetable oil	4 tsp / 20 ml

For the second marinade:

Hung yoghurt (*dahi*)	I cup / 250 gm / 9 oz
Ginger-garlic paste	I ½ tbsp / 27 gm
Red chilli paste	3 tbsp / 45 gm / I ½ oz
Garam masala powder	I tbsp / 9 gm
Dry fenugreek (*kasoori methi*) leaf	
powder	½ tbsp
Salt to taste	
Lemon (*nimbu*) juice	5 tsp / 25 ml
Mustard (*sarson*) oil	4 tsp / 20 ml
Melted butter for basting	6 tsp / 30 ml

METHOD

For the first marinade:
Mix all the ingredients together and apply the paste over the lamb cubes. Rub well and keep aside for 1-2 hours.

For the first marinade:
In a bowl whisk the hung yoghurt and add the remaining ingredients in the order listed. Mix well. Remove excess moisture from the marinated lamb pieces and put them in the above marinade. Leave for 2-3 hours.

Take a skewer and skew the pieces 1" apart along the skewer. Roast in a tandoor or over a charcoal grill at a moderate temperature for 10-12 minutes. Hang the skewer to let the extra moisture drain off completely (2-3 minutes). Baste with melted butter and further roast for 3-4 minutes.

Serve hot with choice of salad and chutney.

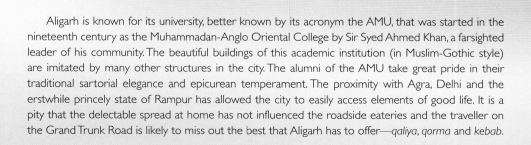

Aligarh is known for its university, better known by its acronym the AMU, that was started in the nineteenth century as the Muhammadan-Anglo Oriental College by Sir Syed Ahmed Khan, a farsighted leader of his community. The beautiful buildings of this academic institution (in Muslim-Gothic style) are imitated by many other structures in the city. The alumni of the AMU take great pride in their traditional sartorial elegance and epicurean temperament. The proximity with Agra, Delhi and the erstwhile princely state of Rampur has allowed the city to easily access elements of good life. It is a pity that the delectable spread at home has not influenced the roadside eateries and the traveller on the Grand Trunk Road is likely to miss out the best that Aligarh has to offer—*qaliya, qorma* and *kebab*.

GINGER FLAVOURED LAMB CHOPS

INGREDIENTS

Lamb chops, cleaned, washed, pat-dried	16

For the first marinade:

Raw papaya paste for tenderizing	4" x 4"
Ginger-garlic (*adrak-lasan*) paste	1 tbsp / 18 gm
Red chilli paste	1 tbsp / 15 gm
Ginger juice	1½ tbsp
Salt to taste	
Vinegar (*sirka*)	2 tsp / 10 ml
Vegetable oil	2 tsp / 10 ml

For the second marinade:

Hung yoghurt (*dahi*)	1 cup / 250 gm / 9 oz
Ginger-garlic paste	1 tbsp / 18 gm
Ginger juice	4 tbsp
Ginger, chopped	2½ tbsp / 60 gm / 2 oz
Salt to taste	
Garam masala powder	1 tbsp / 9 gm
Yellow chilli powder	3 tsp / 9 gm
Vegetable oil	5 tsp / 25 ml
Melted butter for basting	

METHOD

For the first marinade:
Mix all the ingredients together and apply over the lamb chops. Rub well and keep aside for 2-3 hours.

For the second marinade:
In a bowl whisk the hung yoghurt and add the remaining ingredients in the order listed. Mix well. Squeeze the extra moisture from the marinated chops and put them in the above marinade. Keep aside for 3-4 hours.

Take a skewer and skew the marinated lamb chops an inch apart by piercing from the meat and along the bone so that it does not fall. Roast in a tandoor or over a charcoal grill at a moderate temperature for 12-15 minutes. Hang the skewer to let the extra moisture drain off completely. Baste with melted butter and further roast for 4-6 minutes.

Serve hot with choice of salad and chutney.

India / Uttar Pradesh / Awadh

KUNDAN QALIYA

LAMB IN RICH GOLDEN SAUCE

INGREDIENTS

Lamb, washed	1 kg / 2.2 lb
Ghee	2 cups / 400 gm / 14 oz
Onions, finely sliced	4 cups / 500 gm / 1.1 lb
Ginger (adrak) paste	3 tbsp / 50 gm / 1¾ oz
Garlic (lasan) paste	5 tsp / 30 gm / 1 oz
Yoghurt (dahi), beaten	1 cup / 250 gm / 9 oz
Clotted cream (balai), mashed,	
strained	200 gm / 7 oz
Saffron (kesar), crushed	a pinch
Yellow edible colour	a pinch
Salt to taste	
Gold leaves (varq)	10

Masala A:

Coriander (dhaniya) powder	2 tsp / 6 gm
Turmeric (haldi) powder	2 tsp / 6 gm
Red chilli powder	2 tsp / 6 gm

Masala B: finely ground

Cloves (laung)	5 gm
Green cardamom (choti elaichi)	5 gm
Mace (javitri)	2 gm
Black peppercorns (sabut kaali mirch)	½ tsp
Brown cardamom	5 gm
Cinnamon (dalchini)	5 gm

METHOD

Blanch the lamb; strain and keep aside. Carve the lamb pieces into square or round pieces.

Fry the onions in a little ghee till golden brown. Drain the fat and crush the onions into a fine paste with 2 tbsp yoghurt.

Heat the remaining ghee in a pot; add the lamb, onion-yoghurt paste, ginger and garlic paste; fry for 10 minutes. Add all the ingredients in masala A and stir for 5 minutes. Add yoghurt, 1 tbsp at a time, stirring constantly so that the yoghurt is incorporated in the masala. Add a cup of water and all ingredients in masala B. Add salt and cook covered till the lamb is tender.

When the lamb turns soft remove the pieces from the gravy and keep aside. Strain the gravy through a muslin cloth or a fine sieve. Add the clotted cream to the strained gravy along with saffron and yellow colour. Return the lamb pieces into the gravy and cook on low heat for 5 minutes.

Serve hot covering the lamb with gold leaves. Mix the remaining gold leaves in the gravy with a fork so that the gravy looks like emulsified gold! Serve with chapatti or nan.

GILAAWAT KE KEBAB

SMOKED MINCED PATTIES

INGREDIENTS

Kid / Lamb mince	
(minced thrice)	800 gm / 28 oz
Raw papaya paste	6 tbsp / 90 gm / 3 oz
Gram flour (*besan*)	9 tbsp / 90 gm / 3 oz
Salt to taste	
Ghee for shallow frying	
For the smoking:	
Ghee	I tbsp / 15 gm
Green cardamom (*choti elaichi*),	
crushed	4

METHOD

Mix the mince in a bowl with raw papaya paste and reserve for 30 minutes. Add gram flour, mix well and reserve for another 10 minutes.

For the smoking:

Heat the ghee in a frying pan, add the green cardamom, stir on low heat until red, remove and keep aside.

Put a few small pieces of 'live' charcoal in a small metal bowl and place the bowl in a large pan. Spread the mince around the bowl, spread the stirred green cardamom along with the ghee on the charcoal, cover with a lid and smoke for 30 minutes. Uncover, remove the bowl and divide the smoked mince into 12 equal portions, make balls and then flatten between the palms into ¾"-thick round patties.

Heat enough ghee on a griddle (*tawa*) or even a frying pan; add the patties, in convenient batches, and cook on low heat for 5 minutes, turning once.

Serve as a starter garnished with strips of pimentos (optional) and accompanied with raw mango or coriander 'n' mint chutney.

Kanpur today does not present a very attractive visage but there was a time when it was considered to be the most happening place in northern India. It was called the Manchester of the East and scores of chimneys remind us of past glories when this was the pulsating centre of textiles, both cotton and woollen. The city is not only famous for its industry, it was the site where a historic and decisive trial of strength took place between the mutineers and the British forces in the aftermath of the 'mutiny' of 1857. This is where the Maratha rebel commander Nana Sahib Phadnavis took his last stand. He is often portrayed as being responsible for the massacre of hundreds of British residents including women and children. Nana was defeated and was on his way to Nepal to

MUSALLAM RAAN

ROAST LAMB LEG

INGREDIENTS

Lamb leg, washed, cleaned, membranes removed, pricked with a fork	1 kg / 2.2 lb
Raw papaya, crushed	½ cup / 100 gm / 3½ oz
Salt	1 tsp / 3 gm
Ghee	1½ cups / 300 gm / 11 oz
Silver leaves (varq)	2
Almonds (badaam), finely chopped	5 gm

For the marinade:

Yoghurt (dahi)	1 cup / 250 gm / 9 oz
Red chilli powder	2 tsp / 6 gm
Onions, sliced, fried till golden brown, ground to a paste	200 gm / 7 oz
Ginger (adrak) paste	3¼ tsp / 20 gm
Garlic (lasan) paste	3¼ tsp / 20 gm
Saffron (kesar)	a pinch
Yellow colour	a pinch

Gram flour (besan), roasted	1 tbsp / 10 gm
Salt to taste	

Masala A:

Cashew nuts (kaju)	1½ cups / 200 gm / 7 oz
Onion seeds (kalonji)	25 gm
Poppy seeds (khus khus)	50 gm / ¾ oz
Coconut (nariyal), desiccated	10 gm

Masala B:

Green cardamom (choti elaichi)	3 gm
Black cardamom (moti elaichi)	5 gm
Black peppercorns (sabut kaali mirch)	1 tsp / 3 gm
Cloves (laung)	6
Nutmeg (jaiphal)	5 gm
Mace (javitri)	1 blade

METHOD

Apply raw papaya over the lamb leg. Rub evenly so that the papaya juice penetrates the meat. Marinate for 2 hours.

Slightly roast the first 3 ingredients in masala A on a griddle. Then grind the mixture with the coconut to a paste.

Grind the masala B ingredients separately.

Mix all the ingredients of the marinade. Apply on the lamb leg, rubbing well so that it coats the leg evenly. Keep aside for 2 hours.

Add masala A and B; mix well. Place a *lagan* on slow coal fire. Pour ghee and put the lamb leg along with the marinade. Cover with a lid and put a live coal on it; cook on dum for 15 minutes. Remove the lid and turn the leg, cover and cook for 15 minutes more or till the meat is tender. Remove from *lagan* and serve hot on a large platter garnished with silver leaves and almonds; accompanied with bread of your choice.

escape capture by the British when it is believed that he was devoured by a man-eating tiger in the forest. Kanpur was then spelt in a quaintly different manner—Cawnpore. Much has changed since then and many of the civic amenities appear woefully run down in the sprawling jungle of brick and concrete. The foul-smelling tanneries that were polluting the holy river Ganges have been removed by the Supreme Court orders but the stench somehow seems to linger on.

Facing page: Chota Imambara, Lucknow, built by the Nawab of Awadh, Muhammad Ali Shah in 1840.

Food Path: Cuisine along the Grand Trunk Road

MINCED MEAT STUFFED WITH EGG

INGREDIENTS

Meat, minced (*keema*)	500 gm / 1.1 lb	Yoghurt (*dahi*)	2 cups / 500 gm / 1.1 lb
Eggs, hard-boiled	8	Ginger (*adrak*) paste	5 tsp / 30 gm / 1 oz
Cumin (*jeera*) seeds	½ tsp / 1 gm	Garlic (*lasan*) paste	5 tsp / 30 gm / 1oz
Poppy seeds (*khus khus*)	1 tbsp / 9 gm	Gram flour (*besan*),	
Cloves (*laung*)	6	roasted	1¼ cups / 125 gm / 4 oz
Black cardamom (*moti elaichi*)	8	Ghee	1¼ cups / 250 gm / 9 oz
Black peppercorns (*sabut kaali mirch*)	10	Salt to taste	
Dry red chillies (*sookhi lal mirch*)	4-6	Screwpine (*kewra*)	
Onions, large,	3	essence	2 tbsp / 30 ml / 1 fl oz

METHOD

Dry roast the cumin seeds, poppy seeds, cloves, black cardamom, black peppercorns, and 3-4 dry red chillies lightly on a griddle.

Slice one onion into fine pieces, fry to a golden brown colour and grind to a paste with the yoghurt. Grind the remaining onions and the roasted spices separately.

Mix half of the ginger-garlic paste, onion paste, and ground spice powder with the lamb mince. Mix well rubbing in the masalas and the roasted gram flour. Then divide the mince into 8 equal portions. Place a boiled egg in one portion of the mince and shape into a kofta coating the egg evenly. Repeat with the other portions.

Deep-fry the koftas in the ghee; remove and drain. Keep aside.

Heat the ghee, add the remaining onion paste, ginger-garlic paste, ground red chillies, and salt. Fry till the masala is cooked and then add fried onion-yoghurt paste; simmer for about 5 minutes. Stir in screwpine essence. Remove and place in a shallow dish. Halve the koftas and place on the bed of masala and serve hot with roti.

SHAHI QORMA

LAMB IN A RICH SAFFRON GRAVY

INGREDIENTS

Lamb (assorted cuts of 1" piece)	1 kg / 2.2 lb
Ghee	3/4 cup / 150 gm / 5 oz
Green cardamom (choti elaichi)	10
Cloves (laung)	5
Cinnamon (dalchini), 1" sticks	2
Bay leaves (tej patta)	2
Onions, peeled, washed, sliced	1 cup / 120 gm / 4 oz
Ginger (adrak) paste	3 tbsp / 50 gm / 1¾ oz
Garlic (lasan) paste	3 tbsp / 50 gm / 1¾ oz
Salt to taste	
Coriander (dhaniya) powder	2 tsp / 6 gm
Red chilli powder	1½ tsp / 5 gm
Yoghurt (dahi)	1 cup / 250 gm / 9 oz
Garam masala powder	1½ tsp / 5 gm
Mace-cardamom (javitri-elaichi) powder	1 tsp / 3 gm
White pepper (safed mirch) powder	1 tsp / 3 gm
Screwpine (kewra) essence	2 drops
Saffron (kesar), dissolved in water	½ gm
Milk	2 tbsp / 30 ml / 1 fl oz
Almonds (badaam), blanched, de-skinned	20
Silver leaves (varq), for garnishing	

METHOD

Heat the ghee in a pot; add green cardamom, cloves, cinnamon sticks, and bay leaves; sauté on medium heat until they begin to crackle. Add onions and sauté until golden brown. Add ginger-garlic paste and sauté for 2-3 minutes. Add salt, coriander and red chilli powders; stir. Add the lamb pieces and stir-fry for 5 minutes.

Add yoghurt, bring to the boil. Add 3½ cups of water, cover and simmer until the lamb is tender.

Add all the powdered spices and simmer for 8-10 minutes. Adjust the seasoning. Add screwpine essence and saffron; stir.

Transfer to a dish, garnish with almonds and silver leaves.

Kanpur remained in the vanguard of the freedom struggle in the 1920's. Famous revolutionaries like Bhagat Singh and Chandrashekhar Azad hatched many of their thrilling anti-imperialist coups here. One of the major blows they struck was to loot a train near Kakori, a faceless village near Lucknow, whose only claim to fame till then was a shrine of a Sufi saint and a melt-in-the-mouth kebab served to the toothless pilgrims there. The mince for the kebab was obtained from the tendon of the leg of lamb and fat was replaced by khoya (wholemilk fudge), black pepper by white

Facing page: The pretzel-like jalebi, seldom made at home, is often encountered on the GT Road.

NEHARI

SPICY LAMB IN A RICH GRAVY

INGREDIENTS

Lamb chops (*seena*)	8
Shanks of kid / lamb (*nalli*),	
meat on each	8
Shoulder of kid / lamb (*dasti*), 2"	
boned cubes	250 gm / 9 oz
Mustard (*sarson*) oil	1/2 cup / 120 ml / 4 fl oz
Onions, sliced	2 cups / 250 gm / 8 oz
Green cardamom (*choti elaichi*)	6
Cloves (*laung*)	5
Bay leaves (*tej patta*)	5

Cinnamon (*dalchini*), 1" sticks	2
Ginger (*adrak*) paste,	
strained	5 tsp / 30 gm / 1 oz
Garlic (*lasan*), strained	45 gm / 1 1/2 oz
Red chilli powder	1 tsp / 3 gm
Turmeric (*haldi*) powder	1/2 tsp / 1 1/2 gm
Cumin (*jeera*) powder	1/2 tsp / 1 1/2 gm
Coriander (*dhaniya*) powder	1 tsp / 3 gm
Yoghurt (*dahi*)	1/2 cup / 125 gm / 4 oz
Green cardamom (*choti elaichi*)	
powder	1 tsp / 3 gm
Allspice powder (*kebabchini*)	1/2 tsp / 1 1/2 gm
Black pepper (*kaali mirch*)	
powder	1/2 tsp / 1 1/2 gm

Dry fenugreek leaf (*kasoori methi*)	
powder	a generous pinch
Black cardamom (*moti elaichi*) powder	a pinch
Rose petal (*gulaab pankhuri*) powder	a pinch
Mace (*javitri*) powder	a pinch
Gram flour (*besan*), roasted on low heat till	
unique aroma is emited	75 gm / 2 1/2 oz
Salt to taste	

For the accompaniments:

Green coriander (*hara dhaniya*),	
chopped	2 tbsp / 6 1/2 gm
Mint (*pudina*), chopped	1 tbsp / 2 gm
Lemon (*nimbu*), cut into wedges	
Onions, cut into rings	

METHOD

Heat the mustard oil on high till the oil emits its pungent aroma with smoke. Cool and keep aside. Reheat the oil in a pan, add half the onions and fry on medium heat until golden and crisp. Remove and drain the excess oil on absorbent paper towels. Keep aside for garnishing.

Heat the oil again, add green cardamom, cloves, bay leaves, and cinnamon sticks; stir on medium heat until the cardamom begins to change colour. Add the remaining onions

pepper and a new mix of powdered spices which still remains a well-guarded secret. The master wielders of the skewers have since shifted from Kakori to Lucknow. It is well worth a detour backtracking from Kanpur to Lucknow to savour the culinary gems that the city of nawabs has to offer. Much has decayed in the provincial capital of the most populous state of the Indian Union but self-respecting *bawarchis* and *rikabdars* continue to struggle hard to preserve the tradition they have inherited. The onward journey on the Grand Trunk Road can wait a while to taste another lighter than air and wonderfully aromatic kebab that is dished out as *galauti*. *Galauti* is synonymous with the delectable morsel that melts in the mouth. Residents of Lucknow,

MELT-IN-THE-MOUTH SKEWERED KEBABS

and sauté until translucent and glossy. Add ginger-garlic paste, stir-fry until the moisture evaporates.

Add meat, stir for a few seconds. Add red chilli, turmeric, cumin and coriander powders (dissolved in the yoghurt with ¼ cup of water) and stir-fry until the moisture evaporates. Add 11½ cups of water and bring to the boil. Reduce heat to low and simmer, stirring at regular intervals until the meat is cooked and the liquid is reduced to half. Add the remaining

ingredients including fried onions, powdered spices, and gram flour. Adjust the seasoning and remove to a bowl.

Serve garnished with green coriander, mint, lemon wedges, and onion rings.

INGREDIENTS

Lamb, finely minced (*keema*)	800 gm / 28 oz
Ginger-garlic (*adrak-lasan*) paste	1 tsp / 6 gm
Cashew nut (*kaju*) paste	3 tbsp / 45 gm / 1½ oz
Poppy seed (*khus khus*) paste	1 tbsp / 15 gm
Salt to taste	
Garam masala powder	1 tbsp / 9 gm
Yellow chilli powder	1 tbsp / 9 gm
Ghee	4 tsp / 20 gm
Melted butter for basting	

METHOD

In a tray mix the lamb mince with all the ingredients except butter. Divide the mixture into 16 equal portions and shape each into a ball.

Take a skewer and with moist hand spread each ball on the skewer. Grill over charcoal grill at a moderate temperature for 4-6 minutes. Baste with melted butter and further roast for 1-2 minutes.

Serve hot with choice of salad and chutney.

particularly members of the nobility, considered it uncouth to be seen biting into meat or chewing it. The cooks in the court circles were asked to devise delicacies that would avoid mastication. Meats were tenderized by an application of raw papaya paste and for kebab only thrice minced cuts were used. The apocryphal story is that epicures after a life-long indulgence in good life lost their teeth and were forced to resort to such recipes. The person credited with the creation of the famous kebab in the city is Tunda, a cook who lived more than hundred years ago. He was nicknamed Tunda because he had lost an arm in an accident in his adolescence. His recipe handed down generations continues to delight lovers of food with its paté-like consistency and wonderful aromatics. It is not

ROGHAN JOSH

LAMB CURRY

INGREDIENTS

Meat (preferably *dasti* or front leg)	1 kg / 2.2 lb
Ghee / Vegetable oil	1½ cups / 300 gm / 11 oz
Cloves (*laung*)	4
Asafoetida (*hing*)	a pinch
Cinnamon (*dalchini*), 1" stick	1
Yoghurt (*dahi*)	275 gm / 10 oz
Ginger (*adrak*) paste	2" piece
Red chilli powder	1 tsp / 3 gm
Ginger powder (*sonth*)	1 tsp / 3 gm

Sugar	1 tsp / 3 gm
Water	3 cups / 750 ml / 24 fl oz
Garam masala powder	2 tsp / 6 gm
Saffron (*kesar*)	a pinch
Screwpine (*kewra*) essence	1 tsp / 5 ml
Wholemilk fudge (*khoya*)	½ cup / 100 gm / 3½ gm
Salt to taste	
Almonds (*badaam*), soaked, skinned, ground to a paste	25 gm

METHOD

Heat the ghee / oil in a heavy-bottomed pan; add the cloves, asafoetida, cinnamon stick, 250 gm yoghurt, ginger paste, red chilli and ginger powders. Cover and allow to simmer on low heat till all the water evaporates and reddish sediment begins to appear. Stir occasionally to prevent burning. Add 2 tbsp water and cover again. After a few moments, scrape the sediment with a spatula, turning the meat all the time.

Repeat this process till the meat turns reddish brown. Add sugar and water and cook for at least half an hour. When the meat becomes tender, add the garam masala and saffron (ground to a paste with some screwpine essence) and cover for another 10 minutes. When the meat is nearly done, add the wholemilk fudge (thinned with the remaining yoghurt), salt, and almond paste. Place the pan on low heat and cook for a few minutes till the fudge turns red and there is a little gravy left.

only the kebabs that exert an irresistible pull on the gourmet and the gourmand alike; the *kormas* and *salans* cast no less magical a spell.

Lucknow is famous for its *dum pukht*, the art of steam and low pressure cooking in a sealed clay pot. This exquisite cuisine was invented in the kitchens of Nawab Asaf-ud-Daula, when, during a famine, he directed his cooks to put rice, meat, and spices into a gigantic cooking pot, seal it with dough and cook it slowly overnight. This *pulao* would be fed to the poor every morning.

Facing page: The *galauti* is made on the *mahi tawa*. Turning the delicate kebab requires a deft touch.

SHABDEG

LAMB SLOW COOKED WITH SPICES

INGREDIENTS

Lamb	1 kg / 2.2 lb	Raw papaya paste	20 gm
Minced meat (*keema*)	500 gm / 1.1 lb	Garam masala powder	1 tsp / 3 gm
Turnips (*shalgam*)	250 gm / 9 oz	Cumin (*jeera*) powder	2½ tsp / 5 gm
Garlic (*lasan*) paste	3 tbsp / 50 gm / 1¾ oz	Black cumin (*shahi jeera*) powder	1¼ tsp / 3 gm
Turmeric (*haldi*) powder	1½ tsp / 5 gm	Red chilli powder	1½ tbsp / 15 gm
Salt to taste		Yoghurt (*dahi*),	
Saffron (*kesar*), dissolved in 2 tbsp		beaten	2 cups / 500 gm / 1.1 lb
screwpine (*kewra*) essence		Clotted cream (*balai*)	250 gm / 9 oz
for 15 minutes	5 gm	Almond (*badaam*) paste	50 gm / 1¾ oz
Ghee	2 cups / 400 gm / 14 oz	Lemon (*nimbu*) juice	2 tbsp / 30 ml / 1 fl oz
Onions, finely chopped	5 cups / 600 gm / 22 oz	Kashmiri garam masala	1 tsp / 3 gm
Ginger (*adrak*) paste, divided			
into 3 parts	3 tbsp / 50 gm / 1¾ oz		
Cloves (*laung*)	5 gm		
Cinnamon (*dalchini*)	5 gm		
Green cardamom (*choti elaichi*)	3 gm		

METHOD

Roast the turnips in a tandoor till the skin can be easily removed. Peel and prick all over with a fork. Apply half of the garlic paste, turmeric powder, salt, and half of the saffron mixture on the turnips and keep aside for 15 minutes.

Heat the ghee in a pan; fry the turnips to a golden brown colour. Remove and keep aside. In the same fat fry the onions till golden brown and crisp.

Grind cloves, cinnamon sticks, and green cardamom together to a paste.

To prepare the *yakhni* in a pan put half of the fried onions, second part of garlic paste, one part of ginger paste, half of clove-cardamom and cinnamon paste, half of the lamb pieces and enough water to cook the meat to a very soft texture so that it can be strained to obtain the *yakhni*.

When the meat is done, mash the pulp and extract the bones, then strain through a sieve or a muslin cloth. Keep the *yakhni* aside. Then mix the minced meat, papaya paste, second part of ginger, third part of garlic paste and remaining clove-

Lagan ke bataer, musallam raan, band gosht—the list of delicacies in Lucknow is almost endless. And what can match the sparkle of *shahi tukra*—the silver leaf draped, square or round piece of bread with clotted cream, a hint of saffron and slivers of pistachio and almond! It is easy to keep postponing the itinerary but we must continue on our food odyssey promising to return to Lucknow again. *Varq* or silver leaf is the favourite garnish in the kitchens of Awadh. It adorns delicacies both sweet and savoury. No *qorma* or *zarda* or pulao can be served without this crown

Rumi Darwaaza, Lucknow, mute witness to the bygone era of the nawabs.

LAMB COOKED IN YOGHURT

cinnamon-green cardamom paste and ½ tsp garam masala powder. Keep aside for 30 minutes. Shape into balls or koftas approximately the size of the turnips. Deep-fry in the ghee and keep aside.

In the remaining ghee add the remainder of the lamb pieces, fried onions, ginger-garlic paste, cumin, black cumin, red chilli and garam masala powders; fry till the meat is brown. Add yoghurt *yakhni*, beaten *balai*, almond paste, fried turnips, lamb koftas, and lemon juice. Stir

gently. Add sufficient water for a thick gravy and to cook the meat.

Crumble and stir in the Kashmiri garam masala. Seal the lid on the pot with a flour dough and put on dum by placing some live coal on the lid and some below the pot. Let it cook through the night. In the morning, when you open the pot the ghee would be floating on the top.

Add the remaining saffron mixture and serve hot with bread of your choice for breakfast.

INGREDIENTS

Lamb (*raan* or hind leg)	1 kg / 2.2 lb
Ghee / Mustard oil	1½ cups / 300 gm / 11 oz
Cloves (*laung*)	4
Ginger powder (*sonth*)	1 tsp / 3 gm
Asafoetida (*hing*)	a pinch
Ginger (*adrak*), chopped	2" piece
Yoghurt (*dahi*)	1 cup / 250 gm / 9 oz
Red chilli powder	1 tsp / 3 gm
Turmeric (*haldi*) powder	1 tsp / 3 gm
Mango powder (*amchur*)	4 tsp / 12 gm
Coriander (*dhaniya*) powder	1 tsp / 3 gm
Garam masala powder	2 tsp / 6 gm
Green coriander (*hara dhaniya*), chopped	500 gm / 1.1 lb
Salt to taste	

METHOD

Heat the ghee / oil in a tinned pot (*degchi*); add cloves, ginger powder, asafoetida, ginger, meat, yoghurt, red chilli and turmeric powders, and water; sauté for 30 minutes, constantly adding 1-2 tbsp of water to prevent burning.

When the meat becomes tender and a little gravy is left, add the mango, coriander and garam masala powders, and green coriander. Cook for another 10 minutes on low heat, remove and serve.

India / Uttar Pradesh / Awadh

in sterling silver. Making *varq* is a very labourious process where small thin coin-like pieces of silver are placed between layers of leather and paper and are beaten for hours to flatten and transform it to wafer-like foil. Only on rare occasions is the gold or *sone-ka-varq* used. Silver was imbibed enthusiastically in the days of the nawabs as it enjoyed the reputation of having aphrodisiac properties. It is quite commonly used even to drape a betel leaf.

Kanpur city merges into the countryside almost seamlessly into what is known as Kanpur Dehat (rural Kanpur) as the road travels by the side of the river. The *dhabas* here are the places to sample

DHULI MOONG KI DAL

GREEN GRAM TEMPERED WITH ASAFOETIDA

INGREDIENTS

Split green gram (*dhuli moong dal*), soaked for 1 hour	1¼ cups / 250 gm / 9 oz
Asafoetida (*hing*)	a pinch
Turmeric (*haldi*) powder	1 tsp / 3 gm
Salt to taste	
Milk	1 cup / 250 ml / 8 fl oz
Jaggery (*gur*), crushed	1" piece
Ghee	1½-2½ tbsp / 25-50 gm
Cloves (*laung*)	2
Cumin (*jeera*) seeds	½ tsp / 1 gm

METHOD

For the liquid dal:

In a round, heavy-bottomed vessel put in the drained dal and enough fresh water to cover the dal only. Add half the asafoetida, turmeric powder, and salt. Cover and bring to the boil. When the water has almost evaporated and the dal shows signs of softening, add half a cup of hot milk / water / strained rice water, cover again and leave on low heat till it is soft to touch. Let all the water evaporate. When the dal is quite dry turn it with a ladle in a circular motion for about 5 minutes till it is a soft pulp. Now gradually pour in ½ cup of hot water and mix thoroughly to thin the dal. To make it tastier, add some fresh, hot strained, boiled rice water. Stir the dal and rice water slowly to arrive at a fairly thick consistency. Add jaggery and cook for another 5 minutes on low heat. (To give the dal a smoother consistency, sieve it so that all uncooked grains are removed.) Add the remaining milk about 10 minutes before the dal is ready. Heat the ghee; sauté the cloves, cumin seeds, and remaining asafoetida for a few seconds and pour into the dal.

For the dry dal:

Follow the same process as for the liquid dal. When the dal softens and splits, remove it from heat. Add powdered jaggery and hot ghee with asafoetida and cloves.

Alternatively, first heat the ghee, splutter the asafoetida and cloves and immediately add the strained, soaked dal. Fry for a few minutes. Now add salt, turmeric powder, and enough water to cover the dal. Cook on low heat till the dal is soft to touch. Put in the powdered jaggery, and add more water in small quantities, as required, till the dal is quite soft, yet dry.

vegetarian fare that is exceptional. *Nimona*, made with tender green peas, or *sagpeta*, the leafy greens that make the dal a delicacy, are in a class of their own. Talking of lentils, this is the region that marks the *arhar* divide. Beyond the east it becomes increasingly difficult to encounter other dals like *moong*, *masoor*, *malka*, and *urad*. With such a variety of dals one begins to realize that man does not live by *maa di dal* alone. Village cooks, food lore tells us, acquired such mastery over the art of cooking dals that many a time they put the chefs in the royal kitchen to shame.

Kanpur itself does not have much to offer except *Thaggu ke laddu*, the sweet round confections believed to be so tempting that the signage at the sweet shop advises you not to

ARHAR KI DAL

YELLOW LENTIL

INGREDIENTS

Split red gram (*arhar dal*), soaked for 1 hour	1¼ cups / 250 gm / 9 oz
Asafoetida (*hing*)	a pinch
Turmeric (*haldi*) powder	1 tsp / 3 gm
Salt to taste	
Jaggery (*gur*), crushed	1" piece
Ghee	1½-2½ tbsp / 25-50 gm
Cloves (*laung*)	2

METHOD

For the liquid dal:

In a round, heavy-bottomed vessel put in the drained dal and enough fresh water to cover the dal only. Add asafoetida, turmeric powder, and salt. Cover and bring to the boil. When the water has almost evaporated and the dal shows signs of softening, add ½ cup of water, cover again and cook on low heat till it is soft to touch. Let all the water evaporate and when the dal is quite dry turn it with a ladle in a circular motion for about 5 minutes till it is a soft pulp. Now gradually pour in ½ cup of hot water and mix thoroughly to thin the dal. To make it tastier, add some fresh, hot strained, boiled rice water. Stir the dal and rice water slowly to arrive at a fairly thick consistency. Add jaggery and cook for another 5 minutes on low heat. (To give the dal a smoother consistency, sieve it so that all uncooked grains are removed.)

Heat the ghee in a frying pan; splutter the cloves and some asafoetida and pour over the dal.

For the dry dal:

Follow the same process as for liquid dal. When the dal softens and splits, remove from heat. Add powdered jaggery and hot ghee with asafoetida and cloves. Alternatively, first heat the ghee, splutter the asafoetida and cloves and immediately add the strained, soaked dal. Fry for a few minutes. Now add salt and turmeric powder and enough water to cover the dal. Cook on low heat till the dal is soft to touch. Put in the powdered jaggery, and add more water in small quantities, as required, till the dal is quite soft, yet dry.

UNLEAVENED BREAD COOKED ON AN INVERTED GRIDDLE

India / Uttar Pradesh / Awadh

INGREDIENTS

Refined flour (*maida*)	250 gm / 9 oz
Salt to taste	
Cashew nut (*kaju*)	
paste	3¹/₄ tbsp / 50 gm / 1³/₄ oz
Sugar	1¹/₂ tbsp / 25 gm
Milk	1¹/₂ cups / 375 ml / 13 oz
Baking powder	1 tsp / 5 gm
Ghee	5 tbsp / 75 gm / 2¹/₂ oz
Melted ghee	3¹/₄ tbsp / 50 gm / 1³/₄ oz

METHOD

Sieve the flour and salt in a bowl. Make a bay in the centre. Mix together cashew nut paste, sugar, milk, and baking powder in a bowl. Pour this mixture in the bay and knead to a smooth dough.

Divide the dough into 7 equal portions and place the balls on a lightly floured surface. Flatten each ball with a rolling pin into a round disc approximately (8" in diameter). Apply 1 tsp of melted ghee evenly over the disc and dust with flour. Make a radial cut with a knife and starting with one end of the cut, roll the disc firmly into a conical shape. Hold each one between thumb and forefinger, ¹/₂" above the base, and make spiral movements to compress the rest of the cone to make a ball. Keep for 30-40 minutes. Remove, press the ball placed on a lightly floured surface and flatten with a rolling pin into a disc (8" in diameter.)

Place the disc on a preheated *ulta tawa* (inverted griddle), turn once, and apply ghee. Press the disc with a dry cloth from all sides until light brown. Apply ghee and remove. Repeat with the other discs. Serve hot.

offer this to the guests lest they are tempted to stay on for ever. Wayfarers on the Grand Trunk Road are seldom inclined to settle for these *laddus* instead of the *kheer* or the *jalebi* that tickles the sweet tooth equally well.

Facing page: The *halwai* (the professional confectioners) in Lucknow and Kanpur are believed to have migrated from Varanasi, lured by the epicurean Nawab of Awadh (*right*).

YAKHNI PULAO

KASHMIRI LAMB RICE

INGREDIENTS

Lamb chops	500 gm / 1.1 lb	Garlic paste	5 tsp / 30 gm / 1 oz
Yakhni cuts of lamb (*seene ki boti*, *puth*,		Ginger (*adrak*)	5 tsp / 30 gm / 1 oz
neck and *nalli boti*), washed	1 kg / 2.2 lb	Salt to taste	
Basmati rice (one year old)	1 kg / 2.2 lb	Yoghurt (*dahi*), beaten	³/₄ cup / 150 gm / 5 oz
Ghee	1¹/₄ cups / 250 gm / 9 oz	Red chilli powder	1 tsp / 3 gm
Garlic (*lasan*) water	2 tsp	Vetivier (*kewra*) essence	¹/₂ tsp
Onions, sliced	300 gm / 11 oz	Black pepper (*kaali mirch*) to taste	
Cinnamon (*dalchini*), 1" sticks	2	Green cardamom (*choti elaichi*)	5
Brown cardamom (*moti elaichi*)	5	Wholewheat flour (*atta*),	
Cloves (*laung*)	15	to make a dough	2 cups / 300 gm / 11 oz

After Kanpur the next major stop is Allahabad, one of the holiest cities of the Hindus. It is believed to be situated at the confluence of the three major rivers—the Ganga, the Yamuna, and the invisible Saraswati. This is where the famous Kumbha Mela is convened once in twelve years that witnesses an assembly of millions of pilgrims, householders, and sadhus. A dip or ritual bath in the *sangam* (the confluence) is believed to wash away all the accumulated sins. Majestic ramparts

The ubiquitous *chaiwallahs* appears almost miraculously and comes to the rescue of the tired traveller with his readymade brew whenever a fix is required.

METHOD

Heat the ghee and add the garlic water. When the water has evaporated, add the onions and fry till golden brown. Remove the onions and keep aside. Divide the same ghee into 3 parts.

In ²/₃ ghee add 1 cinnamon stick, 3 brown cardamom, *yakhni* cuts of meat, 5 cloves, some ginger-garlic paste, and salt to taste. Cover and cook for some time. Stir continuously till the meat pieces are light brown in colour. Add enough water so as to cover the meat by about 1¹/₂″. Pressure cook for about

45 minutes initially at high heat and then on very low heat. Remove from heat and allow to cool. Strain the *yakhni* through a muslin cloth. Remove the meat pieces. These are overcooked and therefore the flesh comes apart very easily.

Remove the flesh and bone marrow. Mash and strain through a sieve into the *yakhni* to enrich it. To make sure that there are no bone pieces and the *yakhni* is smooth, strain once again. Take chops, remove the bone splinters and loose cartilages, clean and keep aside.

In a pot in 1/3rd of the ghee, add the chops, 2 brown cardamom, 1 cinnamon stick, and salt to taste. Sauté for 5 minutes and cover. Reduce the heat to the minimum and cook. Turn over the pieces in between to ensure even cooking. Cook till done. Remove chops and keep aside. Take about 4 cups of *yakhni* and add to the yoghurt mixed with red chilli powder, screwpine essence, and black pepper to taste; strain through a muslin cloth. Remove excess fat floating on the surface. Check the seasoning.

Parboil 1 kg of rice in water with 2 tbsp of fat that has been removed from the *yakhni*. Add 10 cloves and green cardamom for flavour. Strain the rice through a colander when ³/₄th done; drain.

Arrange alternate layers of the rice and chops. Cover tightly with a lid and seal with dough. Cook on dum by placing slow live coals on the lid. Remove from heat after 30 minutes. Open the lid just before serving. Toss or stir gently once or twice. Serve hot.

of a fort built by the grand Mughal emperor, Akbar, rise from the river bank. Within the fort stands an old ficus tree—the *akshay wat*—which is believed to have existed since the beginning of the universe and can never decay. Allahabad enjoys an enduring reputation due to the quality of the academics and jurists who made it their home in the past. One of the finest contemporary Urdu poets, Firaq Gorakhpuri, spent most of his life here as did the trinity of great Hindi poets—Nirala, Mahadevi Verma, and Sumitra Nandan Pant. And of course, Allahabad is the seat of the Nehru family that played a remarkable role in the Indian freedom struggle and has ruled the country as a dynasty with short breaks for almost half a century. The family homes, Anand Bhawan and Swaraj Bhawan,

BIRYANI

FRAGRANT LAMB RICE

INGREDIENTS

For the rice:

Basmati rice, washed, soaked for 45 minutes	1½ cups / 300 gm / 11oz
Salt to taste	
Rose water (*gulaab jal*)	3 tbsp / 45 ml / 1½ fl oz
Lemon (*nimbu*) juice	1 tbsp / 15 ml

For the bouquet garni (*potli*):

Green cardamom (*choti elaichi*)	5
Cloves (*laung*)	5

For the kid / lamb:

Leg of kid / lamb (*dasti* or shoulder), cleaned, cut into 2" chunks	300 gm / 11 oz
Breast of kid / lamb (*seena*)	300 gm / 11 oz
Ghee	4 tbsp / 60 gm / 2 oz
Green cardamom	5
Cloves	3
Cinnamon (*dalchini*), 1" sticks	2
Bay leaves (*tej patta*)	2
Onions, sliced	½ cup / 60 gm / 2 oz
Garlic (*lasan*) paste, strained	5 tsp / 30 gm
Ginger (*adrak*) paste, strained	2½ tsp / 15 gm
Salt to taste	
Yoghurt (*dahi*), whisked with 1 tsp yellow chilli powder	½ cup / 125 gm / 4 oz
Lemon (*nimbu*) juice	2 tbsp / 30 ml / 1 fl oz
Cream	¼ cup / 60 ml / 2 fl oz
Mace (*javitri*) powder	⅓ tsp
Green cardamom (*choti elaichi*) powder	⅔ tsp / 2 gm
Ginger (*adrak*), cut into juliennes	20 gm / 2" piece
Green chillies, finely chopped	2
Mint (*pudina*), finely chopped	⅓ cup / 15 gm
Green coriander (*hara dhaniya*), finely chopped	¼ cup / 15 gm
Onions, sliced, fried	20 gm
Saffron (*kesar*), soaked in lukewarm water, crushed into a paste	2 tsp / 1 gm
Ghee	1½ tbsp / 25 gm

have been gifted to the nation and are museums worth a visit. Alas, local food is not something that can compare with other attractions of the city. In winters though the guava fruit produced in the groves of the *Khusaro Bagh* are particularly valued by connoisseurs but fewer people have heard of them then those who have of *Dussehari* mangoes of Malihabad or litchis of Muzaffarpur. The local *halwai*, Loknath, does turn out mini *samosas* fried in *desi* ghee, stuffed with a spicy filling of *dal* paste that have a long shelf life and provide an interesting variety of finger food. After the prescribed private round of sightseeing one can press on the pedal to reach the next destination, Varanasi.

METHOD

For the bouquet garni:

Put the two ingredients in a mortar and pound with pestle to break the spices, fold in piece of muslin and secure with enough string for it to hang over the rim of a pan.

For the rice:

Boil 6½ cups of water in a pan. Add the bouquet garni and salt; stir. Add rice and bring to the boil. Add rose water and lemon juice; continue to boil, stirring occasionally, until rice is nine-tenths cooked. Remove and drain, discard the bouquet garni and keep aside.

For the kid / lamb:

Heat the ghee in a pan; add green cardamom, cloves, cinnamon sticks, and bay leaves; stir on medium heat until cardamom changes colour. Add onions, saute until golden brown. Add garlic and ginger pastes, stir for 30 seconds.

Add kid / lamb, stir for 2 minutes. Add salt and stir. Reduce heat to low, cover and cook, stirring occasionally for 20 minutes (add water, if necessary). Uncover and stir-fry until liquid has evaporated. Remove the pan from the heat, stir-in the yoghurt mixture. Return the pan to the heat and stir for a minute. Cover and simmer, stirring occasionally, until three-fourth of the liquid has evaporated. Uncover and simmer, stirring occasionally, until liquid has evaporated and fat leaves the sides.

Add 2 cups of water and bring to the boil, cover and simmer until meat is almost cooked. Remove the meat and squeeze the gravy through a fine muslin into a separate pan. Sprinkle lemon juice, stir, add cream, stir. Adjust seasoning and reserve a quarter to be used during assembling.

Return the meat to the remaining gravy, arranging it in the middle of the pan. Add mace and cardamom powders, stir and keep aside.

Assembling: Return the pan with the meat to heat, sprinkle half ginger, green chillies, mint, green coriander, fried onions, and saffron, arrange half partially cooked rice around the meat, sprinkle remaining ginger, green chillies, mint, coriander, fried onions, and saffron, cover with remaining rice, sprinkle reserved gravy, pour in the ghee and bring to the boil. Remove. Cover with lid and seal with wholewheat dough (*atta*).

Put the sealed pan on dum in the pre-heated oven set at 180°C / 350°F for 15-20 minutes. To serve break the seal and serve from the pan itself with garlic-flavoured yoghurt.

RICE PUDDING

INGREDIENTS

Milk	12 cups / 3 lt / 6 pints
Basmati rice, washed	60 gm / 2 oz
Sugar	2 cups / 400 gm / 14 oz
Wholemilk fudge (khoya), mashed	1 cup / 200 gm / 7 oz
Screwpine (kewra) essence	1/2 cup / 100 ml / 3 1/2 fl oz
Ghee	1/2 cup / 100 gm / 3 1/2 oz
Cashew nut (kaju) paste	4 tbsp / 60 gm / 2 oz
Cream	200 ml / 7 oz
Rose essence (meetha ittar)	a few drops
Green cardamom (choti elaichi) powder	1/4 tsp
Pistachios (pista) and almonds (badaam)	60 gm / 2 oz

METHOD

Bring the milk to the boil; add rice and cook gently till tender. Add half of the sugar. Do not stir until it comes to the boil again. Stir and cook gently for a few minutes. Add wholemilk fudge, little by little, mixing well to avoid lump formation. Add half of the screwpine essence and the remaining sugar. Mix and keep adding the remaining screwpine essence a little by little. Cook until the mixture thickens and sticks to the the spoon.

Pour melted ghee and mix well.

Grind the cream with cashew nut paste and rose essence. Add to the rice mixture. Add green cardamom powder; mix well. Remove and cool to room temperature.

Serve garnished with cream and slivers of pistachios and almonds.

On the way the Grand Trunk Road passes through Jaunpur—a historic city famous for its beautiful mosques and an impressive fort built by Sher Shah Suri. This city has been the seat of the Sharki Sultans, great patrons of arts and music. The region around Jaunpur is famous for its crop of giant horse radishes, some of the marble white roots weighing upto 15 kg. The city itself takes great pride in its

imartees—small pretzel shaped sweets made with lentil flour and filled with mildly sweet sugar syrup.

RICH DESSERT MADE FROM WHEAT EXTRACT

INGREDIENTS

Wheat extract (*samnak*)	250 gm / 9 oz
Milk	20 cups / 5 lt / 16 pints
Wholemilk fudge (*khoya*), mashed	2½ cups / 500 gm / 1.1 lb
Saffron (*kesar*)	1 tsp
Screwpine (*kewra*) essence	½ tsp
Sugar	1 kg / 2.2 lb
Ghee	1 kg / 2.2 lb
Mace (*javitri*)	a blade
Nutmeg (*jaiphal*)	a pinch
Green cardamom (*choti elaichi*)	10

METHOD

In a wok (*kadhai*), mix the wheat extract and milk and cook on low heat, stirring constantly. This process is important to obtain the right consistency. When the milk is reduced to half, add wholemilk fudge, stirring constantly to blend to a smooth mixture.

Add saffron mixture dissolved in screwpine essence and sugar. Keep stirring. When the sugar is incorporated into the mixture and it becomes thick and difficult to stir, add ghee from the sides and stir well for about 20-30 minutes. When the *halwa* no longer sticks to the wok and becomes a cohesive mass, turn it out in a greased tray.

Finely grind the mace, nutmeg and green cardamom. Sieve and sprinkle on the *halwa*. Then mark out diamond shaped pieces and serve when set. This can be stored for even a month in a cool place.

Note: The wheat extract or *samnak* is available at the grocer's or perfume (*ittar*) shop. The method for preparing it is as follows: pick and wash approximately 1 kg of wheat. In a basket spread a moist muslin cloth and place the wheat over it. Then cover with the cloth and keep out in the open in the night to allow dew to fall on it. Repeat this for 6-7 days, keeping the cloth moist till small shoots emerge from the wheat. Now wash and grind the germinated wheat using some water. Then pass through muslin cloth to obtain the extract. This is the protein-rich *samnak* vital for this preparation. It is best prepared on slow wood fire. It takes several hours to prepare but the final product is worth the wait!

Varanasi is the city eternal. The city of light, abode of the great Lord Shiva, manifests here as Vishwanath—the lord of the world. This is the city that guarantees salvation to all those who die within its precincts. This has from time immemorial drawn a huge influx of devout Hindus aging, ailing and infirm, to breathe their last here. Varanasi or Kashi is notorious for its narrow streets, cantankerous widows and slippery steps. However, such slander has never made a dent in its beauty that lies in the eyes of the beholder. The bathing *ghats* and the cremation *ghats* form a large crescent

Pilgrim traffic has always been heavy on the GT Road. The journeys of faith have become increasingly easy.

CHURA MATTAR

BEATEN RICE FLAKES WITH GREEN PEAS

INGREDIENTS

Pounded rice flakes (*chidwa*), washed, soaked in ¼ cup orange juice for 15 minutes	150 gm / 5 oz
Green peas (*hara mattar*)	800 gm / 28 oz
Salt to taste	
Sugar	a pinch
For the rice flake masala:	
Cloves (*laung*)	4
Cinnamon (*dalchini*), 1" sticks	4
Black cardamom (*moti elaichi*)	5
Mace (*javitri*)	2 blades
Bay leaves (*tej patta*)	4
Ghee	5 tbsp / 75 gm / 2½ fl oz
Cumin (*jeera*) seeds	2 tsp / 4 gm
Green chillies, slit deseeded, finely chopped	2

Ginger (*adrak*), finely chopped	30 gm / 3" piece
Asafoetida (*hing*), reserved in 1 tbsp water	a generous pinch
Mango powder (*amchur*)	2 tsp / 6 gm
Sugar	1 tbsp / 15 gm
Raisins (*kishmish*), soaked in water for a few minutes, drained, reserved in 2 tbsp rose water	30 gm / 1 oz
Saffron (*kesar*), crushed with a pestle; reserved in 1 tbsp lukewarm milk and then ground with the back of a spoon, mixed with 4 tbsp cream	1 tsp
Lemon (*nimbu*) juice	2 tbsp / 30 ml / 1 fl oz

METHOD

Pour enough water in a pan, add salt and sugar and bring to the boil. Add peas and boil until *al dente*. Drain and refresh in iced water. Drain at the time of cooking.

For the rice flake masala:

Sun-dry the spices, put in a mortar and pound with a pestle to make a coarse powder. Alternatively, put all the ingredients in a grinder and grind to a coarse powder. Remove and store in a sterilized, dry and airtight container.

Heat the ghee in a wok (*kadhai*); add cumin seeds, stir on medium heat until it begins to pop. Add green chillies, ginger, and asafoetida; stir for 30 seconds. Add the green peas, stir-fry until peas are devoid of moisture, sprinkle rice flake masala, salt, mango powder, and sugar; stir until incorporated.

Add the rice flakes soaked in orange juice and stir gently until mixed, reduce heat to low and simmer, stirring occasionally and carefully, for 1-1½ minutes. Remove, adjust the seasoning, and add the raisins, the saffron-cream mixture, and lemon juice, stir carefully.

girdling the river as it changes directions to flow northwards for a while. *Ghats* like Manikarnika and the Dashashomedha are mentioned in the Hindu epic, *Mahabharat*. However, the present day *ghats* date back to only about a couple of centuries. James Princep was the first Englishman to unveil them for the foreigner through his evocative pen and ink sketches. Unfortunately the river front is revoltingly filthy but a view of the *ghats* from a distance gently floating on barge can haunt the viewer for a lifetime. The temple of Vishwanath, one of the twelve *jyotilingams*, luminescent phallic

The devout carrying their offerings to the sacred river Ganga.

ARVI KE PATTE

SPICY MIXTURE WRAPPED IN YAM LEAVES

INGREDIENTS

Black gram (*dhuli urad dal*), soaked
  for 2 hours   1¼ cups / 250 gm / 9 oz
Yam leaves, medium-sized, washed,
  cut central stems   12
For the stuffing:
Salt, red chilli powder, and
  green chillies to taste

Cumin (*jeera*) powder	2 tsp / 6 gm
Asafoetida (*hing*)	a pinch
Ginger powder (*sonth*)	1 tsp / 3 gm
Ginger (*adrak*)	1" piece
Coriander (*dhaniya*) powder	1 tsp / 3 gm
Vegetable oil	1 cup / 250 ml / 8 fl oz
Turmeric (*haldi*) powder	1 tsp / 3 gm
Mango powder (*amchur*)	2 tsp / 6 gm
Green coriander (*hara dhaniya*) /	
Pudina (*mint*) leaves	a bunch

METHOD

Drain and grind the black gram to a thin paste. Lay the yam leaves on an inverted plate.

For the stuffing:
Mix the stuffing ingredients with the black gram paste and smear this mixture lightly over each leaf. Roll the leaves from end to end to make flat 1" rolls. Place them on a board and cut into 2" pieces; cover the ends of each with more paste.

When all the pieces are done, fry 3-4 pieces at a time till they turn golden brown. Keep aside.

In another vessel put in the remaining oil, add 2 cups of water and boil. As it boils, add turmeric powder and fried yam leaves; reduce heat and simmer till they are tender, but not too soft as they may break.

When a little gravy is left, add the mango powder and shake the vessel lightly. Remove from heat. Sprinkle over with green coriander or mint.

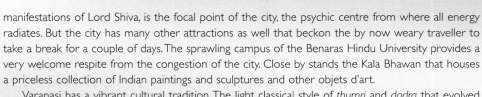

manifestations of Lord Shiva, is the focal point of the city, the psychic centre from where all energy radiates. But the city has many other attractions as well that beckon the by now weary traveller to take a break for a couple of days. The sprawling campus of the Benaras Hindu University provides a very welcome respite from the congestion of the city. Close by stands the Kala Bhawan that houses a priceless collection of Indian paintings and sculptures and other objets d'art.

Varanasi has a vibrant cultural tradition. The light classical style of *thumri* and *dadra* that evolved here has produced remarkable exponents like Siddheshwari Devi and Girja Devi. The greatest *shehnai* player in living memory, Ustad Bismillah Khan, belongs to Varanasi. Other accomplished musicians like

Benarasi Paan

Benarasi *paan* is to all other betel leaves that Darjeeling is to CTC teas, Malihabadi Dussehari to other mangoes and Basmati to plebian rice. This is the *paan* immortalized by the superstar of Bollywood Amitabh Bachchan in the Hindi film song –*Khai ke paan Benaraswaala khul jaye band aqal ka taala!*

There may be loyal patrons of other varieties— *Mahoba*, *Bengali*, *Saunfiya*, *Meetha* or the *Gola*—but nothing matches the mystique of the pale white melt-in-the-mouth *maghahi*. It is the Benarasi *paan* alone that moves connoisseurs to raptures. Other leaves need embellishment—a silver or gold leaf drape, incorporation of *khushboo* or *qimam*, at times the additional support of chutney and *gulkand* but for the king of this realm cloves and cardamom are more than enough. *Launga elaichi ka bida* is the stuff memories are made of. The *panwaris* of the city are called *chaurasia*— master of four (read all) flavours and laugh at anyone who orders anything else at their kiosk. Aficionados maintain that cream of *kaththa* and *chuna* fired in milk are all that this beauty requires to transport you to the realm of sublime. In Lucknow of yore the nawab would keep the *gilori* cool and render them fragrant by packing them in a pouch fashioned with *khus* and drenched with water during the oppressive summer. Nearly each crossroad and street corner has a *paan* shop—and these double as popular rendezvous and rumour mills.

Food Path: Cuisine along the Grand Trunk Road

HING JEEREY KE ALOO

BABY POTATOES FLAVOURED WITH ASAFOETIDA

INGREDIENTS

Baby potatoes	600 gm / 1 lb 5 oz
Salt to taste	
Ghee	5 tbsp / 75 gm / 2½ oz
Asafoetida (*hing*)	a generous pinch
Cumin (*jeera*) seeds	2½ tsp / 5 gm
Ginger (*adrak*), chopped	7½ gm / ¾" piece
Green chillies, deseeded, chopped	1 tsp
Pomegranate (*anaar dana*) powder	1 tbsp / 9 gm
Red chilli powder	1 tsp / 3 gm
Turmeric (*haldi*) powder	1 tsp / 3 gm

For the garnishing:

Tomato, quartered, pulp removed, diced	1
Ginger, cut into juliennes and reserved in 2 tbsp lemon juice	5 gm / ½" piece
Green coriander (*hara dhaniya*), chopped	1 tbsp / 4 gm

METHOD

Boil the potatoes in a pan, with enough water to cover and salt. Cook until tender but not mushy. Drain and keep aside.

Heat the ghee in a pan; add asafoetida, stir on medium heat until it puffs up. Add cumin seeds, and stir until they begin to pop. Add the ginger and green chillies, stir for 30 seconds. Add potatoes and stir-fry for a minute.

Add pomegranate powder, red chilli powder, and turmeric powder; stir-fry until the masala turns dark brown and evenly coats the potatoes. Remove and adjust the seasoning.

Transfer to a serving dish, garnish with tomato, ginger, and green coriander. Serve with puris.

the sitar player Pandit Ravi Shankar have spent their formative years in the city. The creative genius of the people of Varanasi is not confined to music alone. The Benaras School of Kathak, a fast paced vigorous dance form resembling the flamenco that blends breathtakingly nimble footwork and bewildering pirouettes with lyrical, delicate gestures of eyes and fingers to express subtle change of moods, is as exquisite as the better-known kathak from Lucknow. Varanasi for hundreds of years is renowned for its heavily embroidered silk saris, brocades and carpets made in neighbouring Mirzapur.

Facing page: A daredevil youth diving for his daily dip in the flood-swollen Ganga along permanently submerged *ghats*.

Sher Shah Suri's Mausoleum

The mausoleum of Sher Shah Suri at Sasaram is an edifice lacking ostentation but impressive with understated elegance and dignity. The complex also houses his father's tomb. There is a Hindu temple in the background. Unlike many Mughal memorial buildings that followed it, it is not set amidst a lush green garden but is 'framed' instead by a large water body that like a mirror reflects it. Another interesting feature is that the main structure is not perfectly symmetrical but is placed slightly out of sync. This oddity adds to its unusual charm. The solitude of the location invites visitors to reflect on the rise and fall of empires and the enduring legacy that great men leave behind them. It is a pity that the Afghan's most ambitious project—the Grand Trunk Road—is not effortlessly visible from his final resting place

MARINATED CUBES ROASTED ON SKEWERS

INGREDIENTS

Undercut for beef, cut	
into 1" × 3" strips	500 gm / 1.1 lb
For the marinade:	
Onions, ground to a paste	2
Garlic (lasan)	5 cloves
Ginger (adrak)	2" piece
Raw papaya	2" piece
Cinnamon (dalchini)	2" piece
Green cardamom (choti elaichi)	2
Black cardamom (moti elaichi)	2
Black peppercorns (sabut kaali mirch)	6
Allspice berries	6
Vegetable oil	2 tbsp / 30 ml / 1 fl oz
Salt to taste	

METHOD

For the marinade:

Mix all the ingredients together and rub well into the meat. Keep aside for 6 hours.

Thread the pieces of meat though a skewer and pack them together. One long skewer should hold 5 strips of meat. Turn over glowing coals for 10-15 minutes, basting once or twice with oil.

Do not over cook, as the meat is very tender and will fall off the skewer.

Slide the kebabs off the skewer on to a plate and serve with lemon wedges, onion rings, and green chillies.

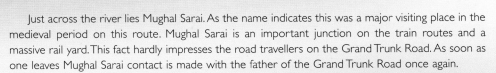

Just across the river lies Mughal Sarai. As the name indicates this was a major visiting place in the medieval period on this route. Mughal Sarai is an important junction on the train routes and a massive rail yard. This fact hardly impresses the road travellers on the Grand Trunk Road. As soon as one leaves Mughal Sarai contact is made with the father of the Grand Trunk Road once again.

Sasaram in Rohtas district of Bihar reminds us to have a look at Sher Shah Suri's mausoleum and a chance to give expression to our carnivorous instincts after a vegetarian spell at Varanasi. Quite an appropriate place to try the *Bihari kebab* an interesting variation on the skewer theme. It is advisable

RABRI

THICKENED MILK SWEET

INGREDIENTS

Full-cream milk	8 cups / 2 lt / 4 pints
Sugar	³/₄ cup / 150 gm / 5 oz
Seeds of green cardamom	
(choti elaichi), powdered	4-5
Rose water (gulaab jal)	1 tsp / 5 ml
or Screwpine (kewra) essence	5-6 drops
Almonds (badaam), blanched,	
sliced	15-20
Pistachios (pista), blanched, sliced	15-20

METHOD

Bring the milk to the boil in a wok (kadhai). Reduce heat and simmer, stirring from time to time, till the milk thickens and is reduced to a third or a quarter of the original volume. (Keep scraping the skin, which sticks to the sides of the pan, and stir it in). This will take 1-1¹/₂ hours. Remove from heat, add sugar and stir till it dissolves completely.

Stir in powdered green cardamom, rose water or screwpine essence, almonds and pistachios. Chill before serving.

REZALA

LAMB AND YOGHURT CURRY

INGREDIENTS

Lamb, cut into big pieces	1 kg / 2.2 lb
For the marinade:	
Onions, medium-sized	2
Ginger (adrak)	2" piece
Garlic (lasan)	8 cloves
Coriander (dhaniya) powder	1 tbsp / 9 gm
Yoghurt (dahi)	2 cups / 500 gm / 1.1 lb
Ghee	1 cup / 200 gm / 7 oz
Onions, small	10
Dried sour plums (alubukhara)	6
Pistachios (pista)	6
Almonds (badaam)	6
Cashew nuts (kaju), chopped	1 tbsp

METHOD

Grind the onions, ginger, and garlic to a smooth paste. Mix in coriander powder and yoghurt to make the marinade. Marinate the meat for an hour in a glass or ceramic dish.

Heat the ghee in a pan till it is smoking, reduce heat slightly and fry the meat along with the marinade over fairly high heat for 5 minutes. Reduce heat and simmer until the meat is half done. Add the onions and dried fruits, and green chillies. Cover and simmer till the meat is tender.

to prepare for the road ahead and stock up provisions because the Grand Trunk Road next passes through a vast, seemingly unending stretch of beautiful countryside through Hazaribagh, Girdih, and Dhanbad, the tribal homeland and a treasure trove of minerals but sadly offering food that can at best be described as indifferent. Local delicacies in this belt are rustic and comprise dahi-chewda (pounded rice soaked in yoghurt), aloo ka chokha (mashed potatoes pepped up with pungent mustard oil), sattu ki litti (a stuffed puri filled with roasted gram or barley flour). A kheer made with shakarkand (sweet potatoes) though is certainly worth trying.

KOSHA MANGSHO

MARINATED LAMB IN A THICK GRAVY

INGREDIENTS

Lamb, cleaned, deboned,	
cut into 1" pieces	800 gm / 28 oz
Yoghurt (*dahi*)	2²/₅ cups / 600 gm / 22 oz
Mustard (*sarson*) oil	¹/₂ cup / 120 ml / 4 fl oz
Red chilli powder	1 tbsp / 9 gm
Turmeric (*haldi*) powder	1¹/₂ tsp / 5 gm
Sugar	1 tbsp / 15 gm
Onions, peeled, washed,	
sliced	2¹/₂ cups / 300 gm / 11 oz
Ginger (*adrak*) paste	5 tsp / 30 gm / 1 oz

Garlic (*lasan*) paste	1³/₄ tsp / 10 gm
Green chillies, slit,	
deseeded, chopped	10 gm
Salt to taste	
Black cardamom	
(*moti elaichi*) powder	1 tbsp / 9 gm
Green coriander	
(*hara dhaniya*), chopped	¹/₄ cup / 15 gm

METHOD

Marinate the lamb with about 1 cup of yoghurt, 2 tbsp mustard oil, red chilli powder, turmeric powder, and sugar. Rub well and keep aside for an hour.

Heat the remaining mustard oil in a pan; add onions and sauté on medium heat until golden brown. Add ginger-garlic paste and green chillies; sauté for 2-3 minutes. Add the lamb along with the marinade and stir-fry on high heat for 5-10 minutes. Add approximately 4 cups of water, cover and simmer until the lamb is tender and the gravy is thick. Add salt and black cardamom powder; stir. Adjust the seasoning.

Transfer to a dish and serve garnished with green coriander.

India / West Bengal / Kolkata

As soon as one reaches West Bengal gates open to a tantalizing gastronomic universe. Burdawan is where the splurging can begin almost immediately. Although there is a popular misconception that the Bengalis eat only fish and only make great sweets, the Bengali cooking is a finely calibrated performance and even the everyday spread makes a valiant effort to balance the six basic tastes and mixes and matches aromas and colours. Fish, of course, is present everywhere but so are a diversity of vegetables. Cooking techniques employed are eclectic from fermenting and steaming to deep-frying.

PATHAR JHOLE

LAMB STEW

INGREDIENTS

Lamb, cut into 1" cubes	500 gm / 1.1 lb
Turmeric (*haldi*) powder	2 tsp / 6 gm
Mustard (*sarson*) oil	4 tsp / 20 ml
Red chilli powder	1 tsp / 3 gm
Coriander (*dhaniya*) powder	1 tsp / 3 gm
Cumin (*jeera*) powder	2 tsp / 6 gm
Ginger (*adrak*) paste	1 tbsp / 18 gm
Water	6 cups / 1½ lt / 5 pints
Green chillies	6
Potatoes, quartered crosswise, fried	250 gm / 9 oz
Sugar	1 tsp / 3 gm
Salt to taste	

Ghee	1½ tbsp / 20 gm
Coconut (*nariyal*), fresh, diced	¼
Cumin (*jeera*) seeds	1 tsp / 2 gm

METHOD

Marinate the meat with ½ tsp turmeric powder and ½ tbsp mustard oil for atleast 30 minutes.

Mix 1 tsp turmeric, red chilli, coriander and cumin powders with ginger paste and water.

Heat 1 tbsp mustard oil in a pan to smoking and pour in the water with the spices. Let the oil come to the surface. Add the green chillies, cover, reduce heat and simmer for 10-12 minutes. Add the marinated meat, cover and simmer until it is three-quarters done.

Add the fried potatoes, sugar, and salt to taste; mix well. Cover and cook till done.

Heat the ghee in a small frying pan and fry the coconut till golden brown. Add the cumin seeds and when the seeds start spluttering, pour this into the lamb mixture. Cover and remove from heat.

This is the city that has gifted to the nation the *rosogolla*—that delightful spongy ball of cottage cheese soaked in lightly sweet sugar syrup and *sondesh*—literally the message—the sweet that is associated with good tidings. Nobin Chandra Sen, a late nineteenth century *moira* (traditional Bengali sweet maker), is credited with the invention of *rosogolla*. Legend has it that not content with serving his patrons the plain *sondesh* he experimented with boiling one in syrup and the rest is history.

The visit to the countryside by the then viceroy Lord Canning inspired another talented kitchen craftsperson to come out with Lady Canning, now *Ladykenni*, an enticing take off on the plebian *pantua*. The last nawab of Awadh Wazid Ali Shah was exiled in this city.

ALOO CHOP

POTATO PATTIES STUFFED WITH MINCED MEAT

INGREDIENTS

For the potatoes:

Potatoes, boiled, mashed	500 gm / 1.1 lb
White pepper (*safed mirch*)	
powder	¹/₂ tsp / 1¹/₂ gm
Nutmeg (*jaiphal*) powder	a pinch
Salt to taste	
Green coriander (*hara dhaniya*),	
chopped	1 tbsp / 4 gm

For the filling:

Vegetable oil	2 tbsp / 30 ml / 1 fl oz
Butter	2 tbsp / 30 gm / 1 oz
Onions, finely chopped	¹/₂ cup / 60 gm / 2 oz
Garlic (*lasan*), finely chopped	8 flakes
Ginger (*adrak*), finely chopped	10 gm / 1" piece
Green chillies, slit, deseeded,	
finely chopped	4
Kid / Lamb mince (*keema*)	450 gm / 1 lb
Salt to taste	

Lemon (*nimbu*) juice	2 tsp / 10 ml
Black peppercorns (*kaali mirch*),	
freshly roasted, coarsely ground	1 tsp / 4 gm
Basil (*meethi tulsi*), chopped	a pinch
Green cardamom (*choti elaichi*)	
powder	a pinch
Clove (*laung*) powder	a pinch
Cinnamon (*dalchini*) powder	a pinch
Processed cheese,	
grated	¹/₂ cup / 60 gm / 2 oz
Tabasco	1 tsp / 5 ml

For the coating:

Eggs, beaten	2
Breadcrumbs for coating	
Vegetable oil for shallow-frying the patties	

METHOD

For the potato mixture:

Mix all the ingredients in a bowl and divide the mixture into 16 equal portions. Shape into balls. Refrigerate for 15 minutes.

For the filling:

Heat the oil and butter in a frying pan; add onions and garlic, sauté on medium heat until translucent and glossy. Add ginger and green chillies, and stir-fry until onions are golden. Then add the mince and salt, stir-fry for 7-8 minutes or until cooked, sprinkling a little water, if necessary, to prevent sticking. Add the remaining ingredients, except cheese and Tabasco, stir. Remove, adjust the seasoning and cool. Add cheese and Tabasco, mix well and divide into 16 equal portions. Flatten each ball between the palms to make round patties, place a portion of the filling in the middle of each and seal the filling inside. flattening each into ³/₄"-thick oval patties. Refrigerate for 15 minutes.

Remove, dip in egg, roll in breadcrumbs and shallow-fry on medium heat until golden. Remove and drain the excess oil on absorbent paper towels.

ALOO DOM

Food Path: Cuisine along the Grand Trunk Road

POTATOES COOKED WITH YOGHURT

INGREDIENTS

Old potatoes, boiled, peeled	500 gm / 1.1 lb
Ghee	1/2 cup / 120 gm / 4 oz
Bay leaves (tej patta)	2
Cloves (laung)	3-4
Cinnamon (dalchini), 1" sticks	2
Green cardamom (choti elaichi)	2
Ginger (adrak) paste	1 tsp / 6 gm
Turmeric (haldi) powder	1/2 tsp / 1 1/2 gm
Yoghurt (dahi)	1 cup / 250 gm / 9 oz
Sugar	1-2 tbsp / 15-30 gm
Salt to taste	

Tomatoes, medium-sized, quartered	2
Ghee	1 tbsp / 15 gm
Green chillies, slit	3

METHOD

Heat the ghee to smoking in a wok (*kadhai*) and reduce heat. Add the bay leaves, cloves, cinnamon sticks, and green cardamom. When these begin to change colour add the ginger paste and stir briskly.

Add turmeric powder dissolved in 1 tbsp water. Slowly stir in the yoghurt (preferably take the wok off the heat to avoid curdling). Now add the potatoes; mix well. Sprinkle sugar and salt and simmer on low heat for about 5 minutes.

Add tomatoes and cook for another 3-4 minutes. Add a little water if necessary to obtain a sauce-like gravy.

Heat the ghee and add slit green chillies to it. Pour into the wok as soon as the chillies acquire a glaze; mix well.

Serve hot.

The multi-layered mince filled *mughlai porotha*, a Bengali speciality, is a legacy from the Mughals. So is the *kathi* kebab, fashioned by wrapping dainty tikka-like morsels in an egg paratha. A small street-side eatery, Nizam's, claims this creation as its own. *Aloo chop* here is not always 'safe' for the vegetarians as it is packed with tasty lamb mince or encases a nicely flattened lamb chop, though the *mocha* cutlet made with plantain flower that bears testimony to Anglo-Indian fusion is just perfect.

Sonar Bangla aka Bengal is more than Kolkata. It is golden beaches, *pokhur* (fish ponds) and much more.

BITTER MIXED VEGETABLES

INGREDIENTS

Potatoes, medium- sized, cut lengthwise into 1½" pieces	100 gm / 3½ oz	Aubergines (*baingan*)	100 gm / 3½ oz
Sweet potatoes (*shakarkand*), cut lengthwise into 1½" pieces	100 gm / 3½ oz	Mustard (*sarson*) oil	2 tbsp / 30 ml / 1 fl oz
		Mattar dal bori	12 small
Drumsticks (*saijan ki phalli*), cut lengthwise into 1½" pieces	100 gm / 3½ oz	Ginger (*adrak*) paste	2 tsp / 12 gm
		Black mustard (*rai*) paste	1 tsp / 5 gm
Bitter gourds (*karela*), small	100 gm / 3½ oz	Carom (*ajwain*) seed paste	½ tsp
White radish (*mooli*), cut lengthwise into 1½" pieces	100 gm / 3½ oz	Water	2½ cups / 625 ml
		Salt to taste	
Plantains (*kacha kela*), cut lengthwise into 1½" pieces	100 gm / 3½ oz	Bay leaves (*tej patta*)	2
		Ghee	1 tsp / 5 gm
Broad beans (*sem*)	100 gm / 3½ oz	Milk	2 tbsp / 30 ml / 1 fl oz
		Roasted *panch phoron* (see p. 135)	

METHOD

Heat the mustard oil to smoking in a wok (*kadhai*). Reduce heat and fry the *mattar dal bon*. Remove from pan and keep aside.

In the same oil, sauté the two kinds of potatoes, the drumsticks, and bitter gourds for 3 minutes on medium heat. Add the rest of the vegetables and ginger paste, black mustard paste, and carom seed paste mixed in the water and strained through a fine muslin strainer. Add salt to taste, cover and cook until the vegetables are done.

Add the *boris*, bay leaves, and ghee, cook for another 2 minutes. Add the milk, cover and remove from heat.

Serve at room temperature, after sprinkling roasted powdered *panch phoron* over it.

India / West Bengal / Kolkata

Anglo-Indian Food

If any one culinary stream in South Asia can claim pan-Indian status it is the Anglo-Indian repertoire. The Anglo-Indian community was scattered all over but there was concentration in cantonments, railway yards, and tea and coffee plantations.

The pure-blooded rulers mostly looked down on these children of a lesser god and found them useful only as an interface with the 'despicable natives', but the Anglo Indians repeatedly dazzled everyone with their unique genius. Their gift for mastering mechanical skills and music were, time and again, put in the service of the land of their birth. This community managed to harmoniously blend the English influence with the indigenous inheritance in the realm of gastronomy. Many a Raj classic—the cutlet, the Dak-Bungalow roast, the railway mutton or chicken curry, fish fry and a wonderful variety of cakes and bakes—owe their existence to their synthesizing genius. Caramel custard, soups and the meat balls and lamb chops, patties and pastries, curry, puffs and biscuits—the list of delicacies that are encountered in remotest locations from the Himalayan hill stations to the coast is almost endless.

Calcutta, once the Imperial Capital of India, is the best place to savour some of these culinary legends that give the lie to the misconception that 'East is East and West is West, and the twain shall never meet'. The city has a formidable array of chops and cutlets including the *mocha*. Christmas and New Year used to be frolic time when all the *box-wallahs* and the planters descended to make up for the lost time. The tradition is still strong to treat family and friends to exotic cakes, mousses, and soufflés.

BENGAL GRAM TEMPERED WITH MUSTARD SEEDS

INGREDIENTS

Bengal gram (*chana dal*),
  soaked in water for 30 minutes,
  drained   2¹/₂ cups / 500 gm / 1.1 lb
Turmeric (*haldi*), soaked in water overnight,
  ground to a paste   1" piece
Salt to taste
Green chillies, slit lengthwise, deseeded   4
Ghee   1 tbsp / 15 gm

For the tempering:
Mustard (*sarson*) oil   3 tbsp / 45 ml / 1¹/₂ fl oz
Black mustard seeds (*rai*)   ¹/₂ tsp / 1¹/₂ gm
Bay leaves (*tej patta*)   2
Coconut (*nariyal*), cut into
  ¹/₄"-long thin slices   30 gm / 1 oz
Dry red chillies (*sookhi lal mirch*)   4
Raisins (*kishmish*), soaked in water   2
Jaggery (*gur*) / Sugar   to taste

For the *panch phoron*:

Cumin (*jeera*) seeds	60 gm / 2 oz
Fennel (*moti saunf*) seeds	60 gm / 2 oz
Fenugreek seeds (*methi dana*)	30 gm / 1 oz
Yellow mustard seeds	30 gm / 1 oz
Onion seeds (*kalonji*)	30 gm / 1 oz

METHOD

For the *panch phoron*:
Sun-dry the spices, put in a mortar, and pound with a pestle to make fine powder. Alternatively, put the spices in a grinder, make a fine powder, sift and store in a sterilized and airtight container.

Put the drained dal in a pan, add salt and 6¹/₄ cups of water; bring to the boil. Reduce heat to low and remove the scum. Add the turmeric paste and the green chillies, cover and simmer, stirring occasionally, until the dal is cooked. Remove and keep aside.

For the tempering:
Heat the mustard oil till smoking in a wok (*kadhai*); remove and cool for 3-4 minutes. Reheat the oil, add mustard seeds and bay leaves, stir on medium heat until the seeds beings to pop. Add 1 tsp *panch phoron* and stir. Add coconut and dry red chillies; stir on medium heat until coconut is light golden. Add raisins and stir until coconut is golden brown. Add the cooked dal, stir until the tempering is fully incorporated. Add jaggery or sugar and simmer until the dal is thick. Remove and adjust the seasoning. Stir in ghee and serve.

Hilsa or *illish maach* is valued above other fish and is enjoyed steamed, and draped elegantly in mustard sauce. *Bhaja*—deep-fried starters—made with myriad vegetables are an indispensable part of a Bengali meal and flavours like *posto* (poppy seeds) lend these a characteristic identity.

Calcutta was the imperial capital before the honour was handed down to Delhi. It was, with Madras, the first place to receive western influence. This is reflected in the food. Kolkata now is more than three hundred years old and very few recall Sootanati, a cluster of fishing villages on the Hooghly river, a minor tributary of the Ganges. Kolkata provides, where the journey concludes, a wonderful opportunity to imbibe myriad influences and please the senses not only the palate. Understandably

KAMALA PHULKOPI

CAULIFLOWER WITH ORANGES

INGREDIENTS

Oranges, peeled, deseeded, pulp extracted	3	Cinnamon (*dalchini*), 2" stick	1
Cauliflower (*phool gobi*), cut into 1" florets	1 kg / 2.2 lb	Turmeric (*haldi*) powder	1 tsp / 3 gm
		Ginger (*adrak*), ground	1 tbsp / 18 gm
Potatoes, peeled, cut into 1" pieces	4	Onions, ground	2
Mustard (*sarson*) oil	4 tbsp / 60 ml / 2 fl oz	Red chilli powder	1 tsp / 3 gm
Bay leaves (*tej patta*)	2	Cumin (*jeera*) powder (optional)	2 tsp / 6 gm
Garam masala powder	1 tsp / 3 gm	Water	½ cup / 125 ml / 4 fl oz
Cloves (*laung*)	4	Sugar	1 tsp / 3 gm
Green cardamom (*choti elaichi*)	2	Salt to taste	
		Green chillies, chopped	3-4

METHOD

Wash and coat the potatoes lightly with turmeric.

Heat the oil to smoking in a pan; reduce heat, add the vegetables and sauté till they are light brown. Remove from the pan and keep aside.

In the same oil, sauté the bay leaves, cloves, green cardamom, and cinnamon till a pleasant fragrance emanates from the spices. Add the turmeric powder, ginger, onions, and red chilli powder. You may add the cumin powder if you like the flavour. Sauté until the spices change colour. Sprinkle a few drops of water to prevent burning. Sugar added to the spices brings out the colour. Add the vegetables, sprinkle salt to taste and put in the pulp of two oranges, reserving the rest for garnishing. Mix well and cover and cook on gentle heat, taking care that the vegetables are not too dry. A little water may be sprinkled from time to time, or ¼ cup of water added to the dish while cooking. Add the green chillies 5 minutes before you remove the pan from the heat. There should be very little gravy left in the pan.

Serve garnished with the remaining orange pulp.

BLACK GRAM DUMPLINGS IN MUSTARD SAUCE

INGREDIENTS

Split dried black gram (*urad dal*), soaked for 30 minutes, drained	½ cup / 100 gm / 3½ oz
Green chillies	2
Salt	1 tsp / 3 gm
Sugar, mixed with 3 cups of water	1 tsp / 3 gm
Ginger (*adrak*) paste	½ tsp / 3 gm
Asafoetida (*hing*)	a pinch
Mustard (*sarson*) oil	1 cup / 250 ml / 8 fl oz
Onion seeds (*kalonji*)	1 tsp / 2 gm
Black and yellow mustard (*rai*) seed paste	2 tbsp

METHOD

Grind the black gram with 2 green chillies, salt, sugar, ginger paste, and asafoetida. Whip for 7-10 minutes with your hand or for 2 minutes in a blender.

Heat the mustard oil to smoking in a wok (*kadhai*); reduce heat and drop a tbsp of the batter at a time carefully so that they form balls (*boras*). Remove the balls when they float to the surface and turn golden brown and leave to drain while you make the sauce. Repeat till all the batter is used up.

Heat 2 tbsp of the oil in the wok to smoking; sauté the onion seeds until they give out their fragrance. Add the mustard paste mixed in water. After it comes to the boil, let it simmer for 10 minutes. Add the dumplings, mix well with the sauce and remove from heat. The dumplings will absorb some of the sauce, but there should be enough left to eat with rice.

the city is dotted with historic landmarks and impressive edifices. The Victoria Memorial is the most prominent, built to awe into submission the natives by imitating and attempting to surpass the Taj at Agra. The temple and the monastery at Belur, where the great mystic Ramkrishna Parmahans lived with his disciple Swami Vivekanand, is like an oasis of peace in a maddening metropolis.

A festive mask used at the time of *Kali Puja*.
Facing page: Howrah Bridge, the old beauty retains its charm despite recent rivals.

POTOLER DOLMA

STUFFED PARMAR IN A THICK GRAVY

INGREDIENTS

Parmar (*parmal*), peeled, scooped	300 gm / 11 oz
Mustard (*sarson*) oil	½ cup / 120 ml / 4 fl oz
Cumin (*jeera*) seeds	2½ tsp / 5 gm
Onions, peeled, washed, chopped	½ cup / 60 gm / 2 oz
Ginger (*adrak*) paste	1¾ tsp / 10 gm
Garlic (*lasan*) paste	1¾ tsp / 10 gm
Red chilli powder	¾ tsp / 2 gm
Tomatoes, chopped	2
Salt to taste	
Garam masala powder	1½ tsp / 5 gm

For the stuffing:

Soft cottage cheese (*chena*)	200 gm / 7 oz
Green coriander (*hara dhaniya*), chopped	¼ cup / 15 gm
Green chillies, slit, deseeded, chopped	1 tsp / 5 gm
Raisins (*kishmish*)	10 gm
Salt to taste	

METHOD

Heat the mustard oil in a wok (*kadhai*); add the parmar and deep-fry until half cooked. Remove and drain the excess oil on absorbent paper towels. Reserve the oil.

For the stuffing: mix all the ingredients together. Stuff this filling in the parmar.

Heat 5 tbsp of the reserved oil; add cumin seeds, stir. Add onions and sauté on medium heat until golden brown. Add ginger-garlic paste and stir for 2-3 minutes. Add red chilli powder and tomatoes; stir until fat appears on the surface. Add salt and approximately ½ cup of water; bring to the boil.

Add the stuffed parmar, cover and simmer until they are tender. Sprinkle garam masala and the remaining green coriander and stir.

Facing page: The Victoria Memorial, built by the custodians of the Raj to upstage the Taj.

KOCHU SAAGER GHONTO

SPICY MISH-MASH OF ARUM LEAVES

INGREDIENTS

Arum, washed, stringed, cut into 3" pieces, soaked in lemon water for 30 minutes, drained	3-4 stalks
Water	2 cups / 500 ml / 16 fl oz
Turmeric (haldi) powder	1 tsp / 3 gm
Roasted moong beans	a handful
Coriander (dhaniya) powder	1 tsp / 3 gm
Black pepper (kaali mirch)	1 tsp / 3 gm
Green cardamom (choti elaichi), peeled, seeded	2
Sugar	2 tsp / 6 gm
Salt to taste	
Ghee	1 tbsp / 15 gm
Aniseed (saunf)	1 tsp / 2 gm
Bay leaves (tej patta)	2
Dry red chillies (sookhi lal mirch)	2
Coconut (nariyal), ground	1 tbsp
Milk	2 tbsp / 30 ml / 1 fl oz

METHOD

Boil the arum in a pan, with turmeric powder and roasted *moong* beans until the dal is soft and the stalks almost mushy. Drain and mash well.

Add the coriander powder, black pepper, green cardamom, sugar, and salt. Heat the ghee in a wok and fry the aniseed, bay leaves, and dry red chillies. When the chillies turn colour add the arum mixture and mix well. Cover and cook until the fat appears on the surface. Add the coconut and milk. Mix well.

Note: When hilsa is cooked into *jhal* or *paturi*, the head is cooked some times with arum stalks. The same procedure as above is followed, only 2 tbsp ginger paste is added with the spices, the hilsa head is broken, coated with turmeric powder and fried in mustard oil and then added to the stalks before it is fried. If the fish head is to be included, the cooking medium should be a mixture of oil and ghee.

BANGLA POLAU

BENGALI PILAF

INGREDIENTS

Basmati rice, washed, soaked for 1 hour, drained	3 kg / 6.6 lb
Water	12 cups / 3 lt / 6 pints
Saffron (*kesar*) colouring	a pinch
Ghee	1 cup / 200 gm / 7 oz
Cashew (*kaju*) nuts	1 cup / 150 gm / 5 oz
Raisins (*kishmish*)	50 gm / 1¾ oz

Whole garam masala (cinnamon, cloves and green cardamom)	5 gm
Sugar	½ cup / 100 gm / 3½ oz
Salt to taste	
Nutmeg (*jaiphal*), grated	½
Mace (*javitri*) powder	1 tsp / 3 gm
Garam masala powder	1 tbsp / 9 gm
Screwpine (*kewra*) essence	1 tbsp / 15 ml
Rose water / Rose petals / Jasmine flowers / Mogra flowers for garnishing	1 tbsp / 15 ml

METHOD

Bring the water to the boil in a pan, add rice and saffron colouring. Let it come to the boil again, skimming off the scum as it rises. Cover and simmer on medium heat until the rice is half cooked. Drain the water from the rice and preserve it.

Heat the ghee on medium heat in a pan; sauté the cashew nuts, raisins and whole garam masala until a fragrance emanates from the spices. Add the rice, sugar, salt, nutmeg, mace powder, garam masala powder, screwpine essence, and rose water.

Mix well, cover with a tight-fitting lid, reduce heat to minimum and cook for another 5-7 minutes by which time the rice should be quite done, and the grains separate. In case the rice is still not quite ready, add a little of the liquid in which it was cooked, cover and leave on a slow fire for 3-4 minutes. Keep it covered until ready to serve, heat for 5-7 minutes before serving.

Serve garnished with a sprinkling of rose petals in winter, and jasmine flowers or mogra flowers in summer.

The eastern metropolis, bursting at the seams, is dotted with a few architectural survivors, the palatial mansions of the old rich. One of these is Jora Sanko where poet Rabindranath Tagore grew up as a child. He is more famous as the first Asian winner of the Nobel prize and founder of Shantiniketan—Vishwa Bharati, an international university.

The Howrah Bridge, for major part of the twentieth century considered a marvel of engineering, has been upstaged by a gleaming new bridge but continues to be a tourist attraction. This is where we

The idol of mother goddess Durga being transported to the *pandal*, the consecrated stage.

TEMPERED BOILED RICE AND GREEN GRAM

INGREDIENTS

Rice	½ cup / 100 gm / 3½ oz
Water	3 cups / 750 ml / 24 fl oz
Split green gram	
(*moong dal*)	½ cup / 100 gm / 3½ oz
Ginger (*adrak*) paste	1 tbsp / 18 gm
Aniseed (*saunf*) paste	2 tsp / 10 gm
Salt to taste	
Ghee	2 tsp / 10 gm
Aniseed	1 tsp / 2 gm
Bay leaves (*tej patta*)	2
Salt to taste	

Optional:

Bottle gourd (*lauki*), cut into 1''pieces	6'' piece
Ridge gourd, medium-sized,	
cut into 1'' pieces	1
Aubergine (*baingan*), medium-sized,	
cut into 1'' pieces	1

METHOD

Boil the rice in a deep pan with split green gram, ginger paste, aniseed paste, and salt until all the water has been absorbed and the mixture is a soft thick consistency.

Heat the ghee to smoking in a ladle; reduce heat and sauté the aniseed and bay leaves until the bay leaves turn colour. Pour over the rice mixture and cover.

Optional: When the *khichuri* is half-cooked, bottle gourd, ridge gourd, aubergine, and sweet potato may be added it.

SWEET COTTAGE CHEESE SQUARES

INGREDIENTS

Cottage cheese (*paneer*)	250 gm / 9 oz
Water	2 tbsp / 30 ml / 1 fl oz
Sugar	1⅔ cups / 120 gm / 4 oz

METHOD

Knead the cottage cheese into a soft granular dough.

Heat the water in a wok (*kadhai*) on moderate heat. Add the sugar and melt on low heat (as the sugar crystallizes on high heat). Boil until the syrup thickens. Add the cottage cheese gently, folding it in with a wooden spoon and stir until it begins to dry. Remove the wok, add the flavouring of your choice and continue pressing the now cooked *sandesh* against the side of the wok until it is cool. Shape the *sandesh* with your hands and press into clay or wooden moulds greased with ghee. Unmould and place on plate.

are told that the Great Road ends but does it? Does the journey ever stop? For thousands of truck drivers who ply on this road everyday reaching Kolkata is no more than a brief stop or short respite to rest and recuperate, then reload and turn back embarking on a journey in the reverse direction, tiring and exhilarating at the same time.

COTTAGE CHEESE DUMPLINGS IN SUGAR SYRUP

INGREDIENTS

Sugar	2½ cups / 500 gm / 1.1 lb
Water	2 cups / 500 ml / 8 fl oz
Soft cottage cheese (*chena*)	250 gm / 9 oz

METHOD

Bring the sugar and water to the boil in a pressure cooker. Stir till the sugar dissolves completely and mixture is syrupy. Strain the syrup. Put back in the pressure cooker.

Knead the soft cottage cheese into a soft dough and divide into small portions. Shape each portion into a ball of desired size. Remember that the cottage cheese will expand with cooking.

Drop the balls carefully into the boiling syrup. Place the lid on the cooker and cook under pressure for 5-6 minutes. For light sponge *rosogolla* remove the pressure cooker from the heat after 5 minutes and cool the cooker with the lid on under running water. This ensures roundness. When the cooker is cool, remove the lid and gently remove the *rosogolla*. Serve hot and fresh.

For the acolyte the Grand Trunk Road is an initiation, a rite of passage. For the veteran it continues to be a test of his endurance skill, the smallest slip can be fatal. For the weak in body and mind, it is nothing else but an unbearable ordeal. For all the food along the Grand Trunk Road remains forever fascinating.

The multi-hued spices reflecting the variety of life along the route.
Facing page: Artisans engaged in making idols of Durga and her children, Ganesh, Lakshmi, Saraswati, and Kartik, in Kumartuli, Kolkata.

ISBN: 978-81-7436-362-6

© This edition Roli & Janssen BV 2008
Third impression
Published in India by Roli Books
in arrangement with
Roli & Janssen BV, The Netherlands
M-75 Greater Kailash II (Market)
New Delhi - 110 048, INDIA
Phone: ++91 (11) 2921 2271 2921
2782, 2921 0886
Fax: ++91 (11) 29217185
E-mail: roli@vsnl.com
Website: rolibooks.com

Editor: Neeta Datta
Design: Arati Subramanyam
Layout design: Kumar Raman
Production: Naresh Nigam

Printed and bound in Singapore

PHOTO CREDITS

Khuda Bux Abro
Amit Pasricha
Shantanu Das
Roli Collection

INDEX